**Other Books by Geri Laing
and Elizabeth Laing Thompson**

Glory Days
Real Life Answers for Teens
Elizabeth

A Life Worth Living
Focusing on What Really Matters
Geri

The Wonder Years
Parenting Preteens and Teens
Sam, Geri and Elizabeth

Raising Awesome Kids—Reloaded
Being the Most Important Influence
in Your Children's Lives
Sam and Geri

The TENDER Years

Parenting Preschoolers

Geri Laing

Elizabeth Laing Thompson

DPI
DISCIPLESHIP
PUBLICATIONS
INTERNATIONAL

www.dpibooks.org

The Tender Years
©2009 by DPI Books
5016 Spedale Court #331
Spring Hill, TN 37174

Poetry ©2009 by Elizabeth Laing Thompson.

Printed in the United States of America

Cover Design: Brian Branch
Cover Photo: ©istockphoto.com/RapidEye
Interior Design: Thais Gloor

ISBN: 978-1-57782-240-0

Contents

Introduction—Geri 11

Introduction—Elizabeth 14

1. Who's the Boss? 17

2. The Instruction Manual 22

3. Mother, May I? 27

4. Stars, Charts and Princess Dresses 33

5. What Quiet? What Time? 40

6. Are You There, God? It's Me, Mommy! 47

7. Sisterhood of the Traveling Diapers 52

8. It Takes a Village 59

9. Still the One 66

10. Wife First, Mommy Second 70

11. Got Romance? 76

12. You Are Special 81

13. The Happy House 85

14. Smiles and Hugs 91

15. Playing Referee 95

16. Superwoman Syndrome 101

17. Dream Job 105

18. Little Einsteins 109

19. Let Them Play 115

20. Discipline Starts Early 120

21. 'No' Is Not a Four-Letter Word 127

22. Broken Record 133

23. The Bedtime Blessing 138

24. Enjoy Them! 144

25. Guardian Angels 149

26. Saved Through Childbearing..........................156

27. Different Pace, Same Passion 160

28. Bless This Mess 165

29. When God Is Your Husband 172

30. The Big Picture 179

Discussion Group Guide 185

About the Authors 191

Poems

Hope Wriggles 10

Wake Up Clapping..32

Room for Two 46

First Dance 58

I Like You Best 90

A Kiss and a Promise...114

Tantrum 126

Soundtrack...132

I Wonder 148

I'm Still Here 183

Hope Wriggles

Elizabeth Laing Thompson

I never knew that hope
could kick fat feet and wriggle,
that miracles with pudgy hands
could clap and squeal and giggle.

I never knew that joy could squirm,
make dying dreams rekindle, burn.

I never knew that chipmunk cheeks exquisite beauty make,
that chocolate eyes and cherry lips could yield the sweetest taste.

I never knew that baby's breath smells fragrant as the flower,
that moonlit-rocking three a.m. could pass a peaceful hour.

I never knew that just one cry could echo on forever,
that seven pounds could outweigh all the universe together.

I never knew how many things in life I never knew,
until the day, oh happy day, when I—at last—knew you.

Introduction

- Geri -

Young mothers today face unprecedented challenges. More of you are working to help support your families than mothers have in the past. The world is busier and moves faster than at any time in history. You are confronted by a nonstop bombardment of information and a torrent of instant, constant communication. Just keeping up with the technology is tough enough. I only had to contend with what I thought was the constant interruption of a telephone extension in every room—you have e-mail, cell phones, text messaging, Facebook and Twitter!

Young moms have instant access to the latest research about everything. You have Internet contact with multiple Web sites, and an overabundance of books with expert opinions on every subject—with child rearing at the top of the list. *Here's how to do it right! Look out for this! Don't let them eat this! This gadget will kill them! Tens of thousands of germs are out there!* It sounds great, and I am sure there is much good in it all, but it can be quite overwhelming.

My desire in writing this book is to help you navigate motherhood with a greater confidence and joy. I am writing from my experience as a preschool teacher, from years of working in the ministry and counseling many women, and most of all, from the experience of raising four children of my own.

Now, as a grandmother, I am watching my children begin to parent, and am involved with helping a new generation of young mothers do what may be the hardest job on earth. I don't pretend to have all of the answers, but I have learned some things along the way. Some things I learned because I watched others who went before me; some things I learned from my own failures and mistakes, and some from the things I did right and that worked over and over again.

Regardless of how lifestyles change, there are two tenets that apply to every generation. The first is this: *God's way always works!* The principles that he lays out for us in the Bible are eternal and can be used and applied to every area of life—always. The second principle? *We need other people to be successful.* The Bible teaches us that the older women are to teach the younger women *"to love their husbands and their children"* (Titus 2:4).Times may change, but people don't. The wisdom and experience that can be gained from godly women who have gone ahead of us is invaluable.

I can never think about the things I learned about raising children without first being humbly grateful to God and for the unfailing wisdom he has left us in his word. And then I owe more than I can ever say to my own mother, Jane Guba, who raised me and my sisters with such love and wisdom. And lastly, I am deeply thankful for my friend, Ann Lucas, who was just far enough ahead of me in years to shine a guiding light for me to follow.

I am so excited to be writing this book with my daughter Elizabeth. I speak as one who has already gone through the years of raising my children, and she as one who is in the midst of it. We are writing short chapters that can be read rather quickly, each centered upon a single thought that can be pondered and considered as you go about your day. We will in each chapter give you some additional verses that you can study, think about, and focus on for the day.

Use this little volume in whatever way helps you the

most. There are enough chapters that you can use it as a devotional book for one month. Our hope is that you can take the things written here, make them your convictions and apply them to your own life.

We speak to you as women who, like you, have been given a great gift and a great task—that of shaping precious young lives into the image of their Creator. These few years are trying, but they are irreplaceable and full of wonder. Although we may at times wish them to be behind us, they are some of the greatest times we will ever have.

Our prayer is that the Father will use this volume to help guide and encourage you as you lovingly, wisely raise your children through the Tender Years.

Introduction

– Elizabeth –

He tends his flock like a shepherd:
  He gathers the lambs in his arms
and carries them close to his heart;
  he gently leads those that have young.
                              Isaiah 40:11

All your sons will be taught by the Lord,
and great will be your children's peace.
                              Isaiah 54:13

If you pick up this book, you'll notice that the byline does not read Dr. Geri Laing or psychologist Elizabeth Laing Thompson. We are Christian women: daughters, mothers and a grandmother (that would be my mom). We are ministers' wives, and one of us is also a mother of ministers (again, that would be my mom!). We are counselors, writers and small-business owners. The thoughts we offer in this book are based on the Bible and on real-life experiences.

My mother writes from a wealth of hard-earned knowledge. She learned a great deal from her own mother, Jane Guba, who bore four girls in five years, and raised them without a car, a dishwasher, a washing machine and disposable diapers. (Yes, you may stand up and applaud now.) My mother also raised four children—two girls and two boys—born over an eleven-year period. All of her children, now young adults, are faithful Christians striving to serve God and people in various capacities. Two are married with children. Two others would love nothing more than to be married, but may never want children of their own after having babysat for mine. (I'm kidding. Sort of.)

I do not consider myself to be a parenting expert! I've only been a parent for a little over three years, and my husband and I are on the Turbo Family Plan, having had three children in less than three years. Our daughter, Cassidy, is three; our son, Blake, has just turned two; and our youngest daughter, Avery Grace, is an infant. The learning curve for us is steep and ever-present.

I write as a young mother fighting to find my way and to do it God's way. The words I write are the lessons that I myself am learning, the methods I am reevaluating, the truths I am stumbling upon every day. While my mom writes with the authority and confidence that come from experience and proven success, I hope to provide a modern perspective on parenting, as one facing the challenges of raising children in the Information Age—just thirty years after my mother began her parenting journey; as one who is living the Tender Years right now.

My chapters provide an amalgam of biblical meditations, wacky anecdotes and practical suggestions for daily survival. I also share some of the poetry I have written for my children during the past few years—poetry that celebrates this precious time of life with our little ones. If my failures and victories can help other young mothers to navigate these rough waters with grace and faith, then my own struggles are not in vain.

We believe that there is no one right way to parent, no one method that works for every child—but godly, Bible-based principles can guide our steps. We believe that God, through his word, other people and common sense, has provided us all with practical, real-life solutions that work.

We take comfort in the knowledge that God is particularly concerned for young children and their mothers. Jesus demonstrated God's affection for little ones when he said, "Let the little children come to me, and do not hinder them, for the kingdom of heaven belongs to such as these" (Matthew 19:14). And as Isaiah 40:11 so eloquently declares, God "tends his flock like a shepherd: He gathers the lambs in his arms and carries them close to his heart; he gently leads those that have young." God not only carries our *children* close to his heart; he gives tender care to *young mothers* as well! He understands that we need special attention and compassion during these years.

This book is intended as an encouragement to young mothers in a time of life that vacillates from heartwarming to hilarious; from exhausting to exasperating—a kaleidoscope of emotions that often hit all at the same time. We hope our words encourage you to walk closely to God, to maintain your spirituality and your sanity, to follow biblical wisdom instead of worldly ways, and to be confident in your parenting.

We also hope that this book provides an opportunity for you to connect with other young mothers. At the end of the book, you will find a discussion guide. We envision groups of moms reading the book together, then meeting to discuss the trials and triumphs of their own journey through the Tender Years.

And so, in the hopes that my children will forgive me for sharing their precious foibles with the world (as I have also forgiven my own parents!), my mother and I offer you our take on *The Tender Years*—ever grateful that God has granted us such Tender Years with our own children. May we all, like Mary the mother of Jesus, treasure these fleeting days in our hearts, pondering them with the joy that only a mother can know.

Who's the Boss?

– Geri –

Listen, my son, to your father's instruction
  and do not forsake your mother's teaching.
They will be a garland to grace your head
  and a chain to adorn your neck.

Proverbs 1:8–9

I will never forget the intense feelings of insecurity and self-doubt that I felt as a new mother. They caught me by surprise. I was the oldest of four children, had been a babysitter throughout my teen years and had served as a preschool teacher for four years. I thought I knew what to expect and how to do this job—piece of cake! Oh, how different it is when you are raising your own child.

As much as our firstborn, Elizabeth, was my delight and my heart, she challenged my authority and my confidence as no one ever had. She was smart and determined, and long before she could verbally express herself, she sensed (and capitalized on) my insecurities and my self-doubt. As Sam often says, "Elizabeth decided to fight for the position of 'head woman' in our house." I found myself debating and arguing with her like I was another two-year-old—and all too often I was on the losing side!

About this time, someone mercifully gave me a copy of James Dobson's books *Dare to Discipline* and *The Strong-Willed Child*. I am forever grateful for these volumes and their author. As I read, I learned that God's plan is for *parents* to be in charge, not the children. I came to see that Sam and I were the first authority that our children would follow and, as they learned to obey and respect us, they would one day learn to obey and respect not only other legitimate authorities such as teachers, coaches and employers, but ultimately God himself.

No, I still didn't always know exactly what to do in every situation, but I did become convinced that God had put Sam and me in charge, and I began to grow in my confidence.

It is amazing how self-confidence changes your behavior. Instead of reacting emotionally, you can calmly be the mother God intended, and take charge. You don't have to engage in arguing and debating or resort to emotional tirades. You said it and you expect it—and that is enough for you and your child to know. You can be confident because you know that God himself has put you in charge. It doesn't mean that everything suddenly becomes easy and your children magically obey every time, but knowing that your authority as a parent is God-given can give you the confidence to calmly follow through on your expectations and to "win"!

You need to be confident, but your confidence is not based on your perfect performance. As a parent you will make mistakes—plenty of them. Sometimes you may be too hard and expect too much, or lose patience. At other times, you won't be strong enough. But none of those mistakes means that you stop being your child's mother! However great you feel your weaknesses are, you still know more than a three-year-old! You are the parent that God has put into your children's life to love and to guide them.

Our children actually *need* us to be confident. When we lack confidence, it fills them with insecurity. They rely on us to feed them, clothe them, love them and protect them. When Elizabeth was still quite young, I left her at home one afternoon with Sam. At that time (thirty years ago!), Sam did not change a lot of diapers, and I rarely used disposable diapers. But hoping to make things easier for him, I left him with disposables. Sam recalls spreading out a blanket on our shag carpet (yes, shag!) and getting ready to change Elizabeth. As she lay there, Sam and a friend tried to figure out how to put on the diaper. Which way did the diaper go? How did the tabs work?

After quite a few minutes, Elizabeth's mouth began to quiver, her eyes filled with tears. If they couldn't figure it out, what was she, a helpless, ten-month-old baby, supposed to do? They had about a decade of college education between them, but they obviously didn't know what they were doing, and it shook her little world. She needed them to at least act like they knew how to put on a diaper! Children may fight us (I've seen many little ones exert their first "power plays" right there on the changing table), but they depend on us for their care and for their sense of security.

One of the most beautiful things about children is their willingness to forgive. Maybe God gives them an extra capacity for forgiveness because we parents need it so much. I am thankful for the many times my children quickly forgave my shortcomings and mistakes. Have you messed up? Have you lost your temper, been too harsh or insensitive? Being confident does not mean we have the right to be prideful or harsh. In fact, true confidence means the humility to admit mistakes, ask for forgiveness and then continue to lead.

There will be many times when you don't know exactly what to do. One scripture that has comforted me tremendously over the years is this one: "If any of you lacks wisdom, he should ask God, who gives generously to all without finding fault and it will be given to him" (James 1:5). Ask God for wisdom, pray for his guidance, and expect him to answer! Nothing has driven me to my knees more than my desperate need for God's help in raising my children.

Sometimes I believe answers literally came to me as I was praying. At other times the answer came through the counsel of someone else or was made clear as the situation unfolded. Especially should you seek wisdom from your husband, the one other person in this world who loves your children as deeply as you do. Also, get advice from other mothers—both those who have already raised their children and young women who are in the midst of these years themselves.

Remember, God's plan is for you to raise your children. As inadequate as you may feel, *you* are the mother and *they* are the children...and *God himself* has entrusted you with this job. You already know much more than you realize, and you certainly know more than they do!

Walk and talk with confidence, not because you are a perfect mother, but because God is a perfect heavenly Father, and with his help, you will succeed. These are "the Tender Years,"—precious, poignant and wonderful. Enjoy your children and learn as you go!

BUILDING BLOCKS

☐ Take out two pictures; one of you and one of your child. Look at them and ask yourself:
  • Which person should be in charge around here?
  • Who knows more about life?

Who's the Boss?

- And most importantly, who has God put in charge?

If you need to, tape the pictures up as a reminder of "who's the boss."

☐ Colossians 3:20
Children, obey your parents in everything, for this pleases the Lord.

The Instruction Manual

- Geri -

From infancy you have known the holy scriptures, which are able to make you wise for salvation through faith in Christ Jesus. All Scripture is God-breathed and is useful for teaching, rebuking, correcting and training in righteousness, so that the man of God may be thoroughly equipped for every good work.

2 Timothy 3:15–16

Have you ever tried to assemble something without first reading the instructions that came with it? I have attempted this a number of times, usually because I was in a hurry, and I have almost always made a mess of things when I did. It looked so easy, so self-explanatory! As my husband, Sam, often says, "When all else fails, follow the instructions!"

Human beings are created by God, and he provided a manual to help us build our lives right. The problem is, most of us think we can do things on our own and that we don't really need the instruction book. That instruction manual for our lives is, of course, the Bible, and I believe with all my heart that it provides answers and guidance to any situation we may face in life. When the Bible is obeyed and its principles and commands are followed, they always work.

What especially amazed me was the power of God's word to help me raise my children. I would say things over and over again to my children and get nowhere (Can you relate?), and then I would open the Bible, read a scripture, and they would respond positively, eagerly and immediately! I do not understand exactly why it works that way except to say that the Bible is "living and active" (Hebrews 4:12). Young moms, more than any other book, the Bible is your best resource.

There are so many scriptures that can be used powerfully to inspire our children, build their faith and shape their character. Use the Bible. Let it "...dwell in you richly" (Colossians 3:16) as you teach your kids. Every principle of righteousness that you need to teach them can be found in the Word. Use the Scriptures to mold character and to teach your little ones the truths about life. You can find a verse or a Bible example to help you deal with any situation, any problem and any attitude. Here are some passages that I used in particular situations with our children.

Jealousy—Genesis 4:4–9

At age five, Elizabeth became quite jealous of her younger brother David. One day I read to her this passage about Cain and Abel, all the while feeling a little unsure whether it might be a bit too strong. She thought about it, looked at me and said, "I wonder if they didn't like each other when they were little?" She got it!

Sibling Relationships—Exodus 2:1–10

The story of Miriam and Moses is a great example to use when teaching an older sibling about taking care of a younger brother or sister.

Quarrelling and Selfishness—James 4:1–2

Do you have children who constantly quarrel or who don't get along? The real problem is that they both want their own way and will fight to get it. This verse can help.

Whining and Complaining—Philippians 4:4

This is one of the first scriptures each of our children memorized, and it worked wonders with unhappiness and whining. It was so effective with Elizabeth that when she would quote it, no matter how upset she may have been, she would always burst out laughing!

'Shine like Stars!'—Philippians 2:14–15

Encourage your kids to want to "shine like stars." Alexandra particularly loved this scripture. She, like many of us, responded best when she was inspired to be better.

Worrying and Fretting—Philippians 4:4–7

This is a wonderful passage to teach children how to deal with anxiety. With it you can teach them to pray about everything and to be thankful. This was a favorite memory verse of David's. He was our worrier. We would talk about this scripture and pray for him to have "peace in his heart."

Anger—Ephesians 4:25–27

Some children have a more emotional, volatile nature. They must learn to deal with things that bother them before their emotions get out of control. Jonathan struggled with his temper, and this scripture helped him tremendously. It taught him to talk about and deal with what he was feeling instead of blowing up.

Laziness—Proverbs 6:6–8

Do you have a child who is content to watch from the sidelines while others carry the load? Deal with this attitude while they are young! Be firm and insist on hard work, but remember to make it fun. Our motto for slow-to-get-going Jonathan was, "Be a lover of hard work!"

Love—1 Corinthians 13:4–7

The most important quality in our lives is love, and this passage teaches this truth powerfully.

⋰

God's word is as relevant today as it was thousands of years ago. Cultures and lifestyles have changed, but human nature remains the same. We have the same needs, desires and insecurities as our ancestors. Right is still right, and wrong is still wrong.

God's word is the greatest instruction manual ever written. It contains all the wisdom we need to live a great life and successfully raise our children. I want to encourage and challenge you: Look to the Bible for guidance and answers to all of life's questions—for yourselves and for your children.

BUILDING BLOCKS

☐ Think of a specific scripture that you can use to address a situation or an attitude in your child's life. Read it together, talk about it, memorize it.

☐ Psalm 19:7–9

The law of the Lord is perfect,
    reviving the soul.
The statutes of the Lord are trustworthy,
    making wise the simple.
The precepts of the Lord are right,
    giving joy to the heart.
The commands of the Lord are radiant,
    giving light to the eyes.

The fear of the LORD is pure,
    enduring forever.
The ordinances of the LORD are sure
    and altogether righteous.

.

Mother, May I?

- Elizabeth -

The fruit of the Spirit is love, joy, peace, patience, kind-
ness, goodness, faithfulness, gentleness and self-control.
Galatians 5:22–23

Parenting sometimes feels so complex—so many character traits to refine, so many lessons to teach. Where do we
even begin? And yet sometimes the simple things go a long
way, much further than we think. I am learning that the
most basic of lessons can plant seeds that blossom into lifelong habits and defining qualities. If you can't figure out
where to begin in training your preschoolers, start simple:
Start with manners.

If your kids already have "please" and "thank you" down,
then be encouraged by your accomplishment—you've made
a great start! Don't be fooled by their simplicity: "Please" and
"thank you" are powerful whine-fighting weapons. Even toddlers whose pronunciation lags a bit behind their compre-
hension can use hand signs.

Once our little ones grasp the concept of saying the right
words, we can move on to more advanced forms of politeness. While saying "please" and "thank you" is a good start,
we also need to teach our kids to use appropriate tones of
voice. *Tone* reveals *heart*. God cares about both actions and
attitudes.

As our kids are getting a little older, we are teaching them not just to growl the word *please*, but to speak in a pleasant, kind tone of voice. When the Imperial Princess demands, "Give me that *puh-leez*," or the Neanderthal yells, "More *peez*!", or if they plead and beg and whine, we make them restate their request until they ask in a pleasant way. We try to keep the exchange lighthearted, but sometimes it takes five or six tries before they get the whine out of their tone.

When they finally get it right, we make a big fuss, saying, "Why, certainly you may have some milk!" or, "Of course! Nothing would delight me more than to cut the crust off your sandwich!" They get a kick out of our ridiculous enthusiasm, but they also get the point.

Blake, as hilarious and engaging as he is, has quite a temper. When he doesn't get his way, his first response is to shriek, yell and injure whatever or whomever is within reach. Some of his frustration stems from his still-developing verbal skills (he turned two during the writing of this book). We try to emphasize key words that we hope will simplify concepts as his vocabulary is still growing—words like "nice," "patient" and "temper." We are teaching him to state his needs calmly.

I have been encouraged to see the change in him as he connects the dots, realizing that screaming does not get him what he wants—but politeness does. He is even beginning to make polite requests without any prompting from us: "D-D-O peez, Mommy," ("Video please, Mommy") and "Chockee meeka peez, Mommy" ("Chocolate milk please, Mommy"). He will even come to me and say, "I nice, Mommy."

Cassidy, in spite of our best efforts, is a picky eater. When I put dinner on the table, she invariably screws up her little pixie face and moans, "I don't want that! I don't like it!"—even if it's a food she has never tasted before. First things first: If we would be embarrassed by the behavior *outside* our home, then it's not okay *inside* our home! We began by teaching her that instead of throwing herself on the floor wailing, "I don't want that!", she should say, "I don't care for any of that, thank you."

Now that she's a little older, we are taking it a step further. Our friends Spencer and Brianne gave us the idea for the "no-thank-you bite": She doesn't have to clean her plate—I don't think I could force her to swallow unwanted food even with a pair of pliers and a shovel—but she does have to take one bite. If she still doesn't like the food, she can just say, "No thank you," and we move on.

Manners begin at home, but need to extend to people outside the family, too. Friendliness is a difficult lesson for many toddlers, but is one we can't ignore. If we aren't careful, behavior that we write off now as mere shyness or insecurity (and that we even think is cute!) can later morph into snobbishness and unkindness. Friendliness starts with just saying hello and good-bye.

Nowhere is this more challenging for my kids than at church. They are tired and hungry after class, and everyone knows who they are, being the children of the campus minister and the grandchildren of the preacher! I try not to ask for trouble by inflicting extensive fellowship time on tired toddlers. However, we don't let them get away with rude behavior like scowling at people, burying their heads in our shoulders, or even coyness that is really just unfriendliness in disguise. They need to smile and either wave or say hello, depending on their vocal abilities. When one of my kids is rude to someone at church (or elsewhere), my mom has taught me to take the child off to the side, have a talk, then bring them back to try their greeting again (and sometimes to apologize, if necessary).

Our church and family are very huggy, but we don't force our kids to hug. Blake is especially wary of unfamiliar people, but he likes to play "high five," so we encourage him to give high fives as his form of a friendly greeting.

Kevin and I want our kids to understand that adults deserve respect, and so we don't allow them to call grown-ups simply by their first names: Family friends are "Mr. Joe" and "Mrs. Laura." I realize that our practice may feel old-fashioned or awkward for some people in today's casual society, but however you choose to approach it, the lesson of respecting elders and authority is essential.

As with most parenting strategies, we'll have much better luck if we practice the respect and manners that we preach. How do we address our husbands or other family members, even when life is hectic? How humbling it is to hear a preschooler parrot back our own sharp tone or careless words! I try to keep an impatient edge out of my voice, even when I am exhausted and stretched to my limit (and yes, I sometimes fail, and then it is Mommy's turn to apologize!). That *doesn't* mean that I cannot speak firmly or even raise my voice to get my children's attention when necessary, but I want most of my words and tone to exude compassion and patience.

As silly as it sounds, I even have to be careful how I speak to our dog! Our Labrador retriever Cole, my shadow and fourth child, has a gift for positioning himself in the worst possible places; I nearly break my neck tripping over him at least once a week. It's so tempting to yell at him or to nudge him out of the way, muttering, "Dumb dog." But as Laura Ingalls Wilder put it in *Little House on the Prairie*, "Little pitchers have big ears," and my kids imitate anything I say and do. Already they point their fingers at the dog and state garbled commands to sit and stay—but I have also overheard them politely say, "Excuse me, Cole!"

Good manners are not just about being polite or impressing senior citizens; they lay the foundation for the more important heart lessons of respect, self-control, gratitude and love. As with every facet of parenting, teaching manners is both easier *and* harder than we think—but we will reap the dividends of our investment for the rest of our lives. Who knew that you could get so much mileage out of "please" and "thank you"? Maybe they really are "magic words" after all!

BUILDING BLOCKS

☐ Want a fun idea for a toddler-friendly family devotional? We recently based a devotional on Proverbs 16:24: "Pleasant words are a honeycomb, sweet to the soul and healing to the bones." After reading the scripture, we practiced saying "sweet" words, and every time our kids came up with a kind thing to say (like, "Blakey, can you please share that toy with me?" or "Thank you for sharing, Cassie"), we gave them a taste of honey. Then we told them to come up with examples of "sour" words, and gave them a taste of lemon juice. The kids talked about sweet and sour words for weeks afterward!

☐ Colossians 4:6
Let your conversation be always full of grace, seasoned with salt, so that you may know how to answer everyone.

Wake Up Clapping

Elizabeth Laing Thompson

I learned a life lesson this morning at dawn
As I started to wake with a groan and a yawn.
Tossing and dreading the start of a day,
I pulled up the covers, just longing to stay.

From o'er in the crib I heard *slap-slap-slap*,
As two happy hands, they started to clap;
Listening and thinking, I lay for a while,
Suddenly starting my day with a smile.
This morning I learned from a ten-month-old girl
To start each day fresh, open wide to the world:

Greet each new morn with a laugh and a song,
Rejoice with the hope of what might come along;
Applaud the sunrise; cheer day's first light;
Celebrate living through yet one more night.
When birds chirp their thanks, join in with their singing,
Give thanks to God for the blessings he's bringing.

Who knew that great wisdom—now isn't it wild—
Could come from the mouth—or the hands—of a child?
And so now each day, after night's too-short napping,
I, like my baby, wake up and start clapping.

Stars, Charts and Princess Dresses

– Elizabeth –

He who scorns instruction will pay for it,
but he who respects a command is rewarded.

Proverbs 13:13

Have you noticed that political correctness is now ridding the world of One Size Fits All clothing? Now it's One Size Fits Most. What?! Are manufacturers afraid someone will sue them for false advertising and self-esteem damage if a sweater doesn't fit? If we're really striving for honesty, let's go all the way: "One Size Makes Small People Look Like Mr. Potato Head and Shapely People Look Like Tweedledee."

If One Size Fits All never worked that well for clothing, why would we expect it to work for parenting? There is no One Size Fits All method of discipline. In my three whopping years of parenting experience, I have already realized that the perfect solution for one child does little for another. Successful parenting takes an immense amount of creativity and thought.

Do you ever feel that you have exhausted every avenue of discipline? Chances are, you haven't! If spankings and Time Outs are the only things in our discipline repertoire, a clever or stubborn child will quickly stymie us. By remaining open to new methods, we will grow in our parenting, all the while keeping step with our children's maturation and progress.

Watching our kids and studying their personalities will help us to devise more effective rewards and consequences for each individual. Because life moves at such a frenetic pace when our children are young, we have to stay on our game mentally, and not check out because we are tired or distracted. (And just think: They aren't even preteens yet! Aaaaah!)

I am learning that I can't be afraid to experiment with a new strategy, tweak it over time, and try something else if it doesn't work. Of course our kids need consistent consequences when they cross certain lines—they will *always* hit the same immovable fence when they try to hit or bite or lie—but sometimes they need new *positive* motivations as well.

This is no new teaching: God has modeled creative and multi-faceted discipline for us from the beginning! He metes out punishment for rebellion, tempered by reward and fatherly affection; thus he has always inspired a masterful balance of healthy fear and loving devotion. In Deuteronomy 30:19–20 he says,

> This day I call heaven and earth as witnesses against you that I have set before you life and death, blessings and curses. Now choose life, so that you and your children may live and that you may love the LORD your God, listen to his voice, and hold fast to him. For the LORD is your life, and he will give you many years in the land he swore to give to your fathers, Abraham, Isaac and Jacob.

Now if only I were as smart as God...

Cassidy, being exceptionally bright, keeps me on my parenting toes. Sometimes I can almost see the wheels turning behind her obsidian eyes as she tries to devise a way to stump me. And sometimes, she does! But Kevin and I have figured out a few methods that keep us a step ahead of her. We learned early on that she loves working for rewards. Like her mother, she is a highly motivated person who loves the feeling of accomplishment...and the taste of chocolate.

When Cassidy was about eighteen months old, she began throwing tantrums whenever we left the park or restaurant playgrounds. Every mother knows the awful humiliation as your adorable child, who received glowing compliments from the other customers as you first entered the restaurant, now makes you look like an inept idiot as she screams and hits and pulls your hair when it is time to leave.

And what are you supposed to do? Create an even more dramatic scene by screaming back? Or smack her hand and risk getting hauled off to jail for child abuse? I quickly realized that if I ever wanted to take her out in public again, I needed a game plan.

I turned to my trusty friend: chocolate. Before we even left home on our way to fun places, I began telling Cassidy that I had some chocolate packed in my bag for her (usually two or three M&Ms or chocolate chips), and that she could have them on the ride home as a reward for getting back into the car happily.

Sure, you could call it a bribe—I preferred to think of it as a reward—but it worked beautifully. The advance warning helped her decide to cooperate ahead of time, so she was mentally prepared when it was time to leave. Within a few months, as her self-control grew, she began leaving fun places with a good attitude, chocolate or no chocolate.

This experience taught me that I always have to stay one

step ahead of my kids—to anticipate their feelings and behavior, so that I am prepared. When I am unprepared, heaven help me...and anyone else unfortunate enough to be in the blast zone!

Now that Cassidy is three-going-on-twelve, it often takes more than a few pieces of chocolate to win her over. A few weeks after her third birthday (when the terrible twos were supposed to be over!), she began pitching horrible fits at bedtime and naptime—the kind where you are afraid they are going to throw up, have a seizure or choke to death on their own tears. Like a possessed Energizer Bunny, she kept screaming, and screaming, and screaming...

Soon her rebellious bedtime attitude began spilling over into every other area of life, turning the most simple interactions into power struggles. After two weeks of all-out warfare, I was at my wits' end.

Punishments didn't make much of a dent in her armor. In desperation, we decided to employ a strategy that I am told worked wonders with me when I was three: the Star Chart. We introduced the idea to Cassidy by reading Philippians 2:14–16: "Do everything without complaining or arguing, so that you may...shine like stars in the universe as you hold out the word of life." We talked about what it means to shine like a star, and practiced ways to shine like a star and ways not to shine like a star. Afterwards, we made a big deal of decorating a Shine Like a Star Chart together.

At the end of every day, Cassidy would receive a star sticker if she got dressed happily; went potty happily; got in the car seat happily; shared with Blake; took a nap happily; obeyed the first time; brushed her teeth happily; and went to bed happily. Her reward when she completed the chart would be the Holy Grail of princess wannabes: a pink and purple Ariel princess dress. (Whether such a dress existed, I knew not—but I would get one custom made if I had to!)

Filling out the star chart became a new, exciting part of our bedtime ritual. (An unexpected side benefit of this exercise was that it reminded *me* of how many victories Cassidy had achieved throughout the day, so I did not focus only on one or two episodes of misbehavior.)

My little Type A girl latched on to her goal with intensity and enthusiasm. On the very first day, bedtime became once more a fun, bonding time, instead of a grueling standoff. And the consistent nature of the chart helped to break her emerging cycle of defiance before it took firm root, and established a new routine—a new normal.

By the time Cassidy finished with the chart weeks later, she was a different kid. Not only did bedtime improve, but her overall attitude about obedience and cooperation got better, too. The Star Chart retrained her behavior *and* her heart.

When the chart was complete, we made a HUGE deal out of it. We bragged about Cassidy's hard-earned victory to all of our friends and family, and Cassidy glowed with a healthy pride the whole time. We picked out the dress she wanted online, and stalked the mailman every day until it arrived. And then when it showed up on the doorstep, we had a Princess Day to celebrate.

Cassidy dressed up in her new "dress" (actually a nightgown!), my mom braved a morning alone with my other two kids, and I took Cassidy out on the town to get a manicure and eat a Princess Dessert. It was one of our best Mommy-and-me memories; a well-deserved celebration not only of Cassidy's improved behavior, but of her new spirit as well.

We *all* grew a lot from the experience: Cassidy changed and matured, and Kevin and I gained insight in how to help her learn, and how to parent "outside the box"—but inside the heart.

Even after the Star Chart victory, Cassidy needed some ongoing motivation for cooperating at bedtime. We followed up on the Star Chart with another strategy, adapted from a method my friend Heather has used—and of course, the Thompson version involves chocolate. (What can I say? We really love our chocolate.)

Every night, we put five M&Ms on a napkin in Cassidy's room. Her goal is to keep all five pieces so that she can eat them in the morning. Every time she is uncooperative or calls us back into her room after she's already in bed, she loses an M&M. We like this straightforward strategy because its non-negotiable nature eliminates arguments and power struggles, and keeps us from feeling like the bad guys: "You need another sip of water? You want socks on? Okay, but if I come back into your room, you lose another M&M—those are the rules!" Most nights, Cassidy now keeps all her candy—and as a side benefit, she can now subtract really well!

Someone once said, "If all you have is a hammer, everything looks like a nail." Moms, let's put our beleaguered brains to work, and invent some creative and positive ways to shape the minds and hearts of our little ones.

BUILDING BLOCKS

☐ Watch and study each of your children today. What character trait does each child need to focus on right now? Are they more motivated by consequences or by reward? What do they love the most? What positive motivations could inspire them? What would hurt the most if it were taken away as a consequence?

☐ Psalm 62:11–12
One thing God has spoken,
two things have I heard:
that you, O God, are strong,
and that you, O LORD, are loving.
Surely you will reward each person
according to what he has done.

What Quiet? What Time?

- Elizabeth -

As the deer pants for streams of water,
     so my soul pants for you, O God.
My soul thirsts for God, for the living God.
     When can I go and meet with God?
My [children's] tears have been my food day and night.
          Psalm 42:1–3, ETV—Elizabeth Thompson Version

Ah, the glorious days of old, when I could set aside an hour every day to spend in peaceful meditation and communion with God—my "quiet times." The concepts of *quiet* and *time* now exist in my vocabulary only as distant memories, two long-lost friends that I imagine will return to my life one day—but not any day soon! I went from feasting on the Word, to a virtual famine, in a very short time (well, in nine-and-a-half months, to be exact).

When we have children, nurturing our "walk with God" takes on a much more literal connotation. These days, my relationship with God really does develop as I am walking (or, more accurately, as I am running after a rebellious child in a parking lot; or folding laundry during naptime; or chopping vegetables for dinner while sticking a pacifier in a baby's mouth and dancing with a three-year-old and teaching a two-year-old to say "please")—because I rarely have time to sit with God!

And yet, now that we are mothers, we still need to be

close to God, perhaps even *more* desperately than we did in our more flexible days. We have days when our patience is stretched so thin it nearly disappears; times when we feel alone and trapped in a house that seems smaller by the minute; moments when we question our ability to raise our little Tasmanian devils in a godly way.

We all know that if we neglect our relationship with God, it will wither and our spiritual senses will grow dull. We do not want to find that, in the process of raising our children, we are losing the passionate faith we hope to pass on to them. Our goal should be to exemplify such an inspiring walk with God that our kids desire a relationship of their own one day. I always remember seeing both of my parents disappear behind their study doors every morning, for time with God— and as I grew older, I imitated their habit, a practice that I want to pass on to my own family. I may be a very imperfect mother and Christian, but I can at least set an example for my children in my daily spiritual disciplines.

Although I do not claim to be a stellar example of daily devotional time with God at this point in my life, I have not given up—I am still fighting to walk with him. Indeed, one of our aims in writing this book is to provide young moms with what could be a month's worth of daily readings—easily digestible inspirations, spiritual truths and practical lessons that you can read in five or ten minutes and take with you even on the busiest of days.

Over the past few years of my journey into motherhood, I have discovered some strategies that have made my walk with God possible—and even enjoyable. Several godly friends have taught me some of their methods, too, and I hope our collective ideas may help other new mothers to remain close to God.

I love Psalm 42:8, where David says, "By day the Lord directs his love, at night his song is with me—a prayer to the God of my life." Not only does God send his love our way during the hectic daytime hours, but he is with us through the long nights as well. How many nights do we spend awake, nursing a newborn or rocking a sick child? Sometimes those night hours, when the house is quiet except for us and our babies, afford a precious opportunity to connect with God. As Psalm 63:6 puts it,

> On my bed I remember you;
> > I think of you through the watches of the night.
> Because you are my help,
> > I sing in the shadow of your wings.

(Thanks to my Grandma for the inspiration behind this suggestion!)

I think often of the scripture in Deuteronomy 6:5–9, where God says,

> Love the LORD your God with all your heart and with all your soul and with all your strength. These commandments that I give you today are to be upon your hearts. Impress them on your children. Talk about them when you sit at home and when you walk along the road, when you lie down and when you get up. Tie them as symbols on your hands and bind them on your foreheads. Write them on the doorframes of your houses and on your gates.

I am learning to bring God into the everyday moments of life, and to keep his word accessible both in my heart and in my home.

I have learned to take advantage of time whenever it presents itself. I may not always find fifteen consecutive minutes to sit and talk to God, but many days I manage to pray for that long, in short intervals ranging from two to ten minutes. I pray when I nurse the baby; when I drive and the children are strapped in and unable to harm themselves or anyone else; when the stars align and everyone sleeps at the same time for a few blessed minutes. Sometimes I'll put the kids in the stroller and attempt a prayer walk around the neighborhood.

I now keep a Bible handy in the kitchen and in my diaper bag so that if a free moment surprises me either at home or while I am waiting for an appointment, I can read.

Since my times are so limited, I love keeping a spiritual book handy, alongside my Bible—a little like having a microwaveable meal. If I find five minutes to read, I just grab the book, pop its contents in my brain, and *voila!*—spiritual truths are easy to read and ingest. I rarely have time to sit down, figure out what to study, and do an in-depth analysis. It helps to have spiritual insights already written out for me. When I am not reading a spiritual book, I like to have a Bible reading plan. This year I am reading through a chronological Bible divided into daily readings, and it is so helpful to have a ready-made Bible study waiting for me every day. (I confess, I am woefully behind, but plodding along anyway.)

As my oldest daughter has turned three, she can entertain herself for short periods of time. And yet, if she catches me reading my Bible in the kitchen, she immediately begins making demands. I have recently begun to set a timer for ten minutes, telling her that I am having my quiet time, and that I will be available to help her when the timer goes off. Magically, this works! She leaves the room, finds something to do, and comes back in when she hears the timer go off. (Thanks, Sarah, for the idea!)

On occasion, I ask my husband to give me twenty minutes to myself. I grab a cup of coffee and a Bible, run into a quiet room, and boy, can I get a lot out of a twenty-minute break with God! I always come out singing and at peace—much better prepared for a day of caring for my little zoo. (And thanks go to Sara and Melissa for this suggestion.)

If you can get all of your children on the same nap schedule, you will probably find yourself with an hour and a half—maybe even two or three hours, I kid you not!—in which you can spend time with God, take a nap, work out, return e-mails, speed clean your house, prepare dinner, and perhaps have five minutes left over to stare at the walls, savoring the sound of silence.

If you just can't find a consistent daily time with God, try setting aside a longer time at least once every week or so—like a mini-date with God—to sustain you during the chaos of everyday life. You may have to get up at the crack of dawn to make it happen, but the loss of sleep will be worth the spiritual renewal. It's not as if you're sleeping much anyway, right?

In the meantime, let's all learn to rely on God's grace and not berate ourselves for being horrible Christians if we can't spend as much time with God as we used to—while also challenging ourselves to be creative and make opportunities whenever we can. This stage of life is temporary, and one day we will be able to have consistent, lengthy times with God again.

I look forward to that day. But until then, I am going to walk with God, even if he has to run to keep up!

BUILDING BLOCKS

☐ How can you make it easier to spend time with God when you have unexpected free time? Try planting Bibles or spiritual books in key places throughout your home, or writing scriptures on note cards that you carry in your pocket throughout the day.

☐ Psalm 119:62, 97
At midnight I rise to give you thanks
    for your righteous laws....
Oh, how I love your law!
    I meditate on it all day long.

Room for Two

Elizabeth Laing Thompson

Miniature hat—dwarfed by the palm of my hand,
For a head that has never seen the sun;
Diapers—impossibly, laughably small,
For a little bottom that likes to play bumper cars with my ribs;
Tiny socks, tucked next to mine,
For toes that have never felt the cool, almost-spring air.
I hold them up, chuckle...but then I think,
If I don't pack you socks, who will?
In a rush, the weight hits me—the profound, couched in the mundane:

> Your feet, cold and tinged with blue, will be mine to warm;
> Your body, unfathomably small, mine to clothe;
> Your bottom, baby soft as they say, mine to diaper;
> Your life, priceless and unwritten, mine to guide;
> Your heart, never wounded, never betrayed, mine to protect.

Alone but together, I check in: "Room for two, please."
In the corner, your pint-sized bed waits.

Check-in as one, check-out as two:
No instruction manual, no warranty, no receipt for return or exchange,
Just a smile and "Congratulations! Good luck!"
And a balloon.

Ride for two:
We roll out to greet the wide wondrous whelming hope-saturated universe.
Two lives, forever entwined, blinking in the welcoming sun.
I sigh, the weight of the world, a shiny new life, cradled in my arms.
Silently, I pray that the world will make room for two—room for you.

Are You There, God? It's Me, Mommy!

– Geri –

> By day the Lord directs his love,
> at night his song is with me
> a prayer to the God of my life.
>
> Psalm 42:8

When Elizabeth was quite young, she became aware of a terrible famine that was killing thousands of children in Ethiopia. The thought that children like her were dying because they didn't have enough to eat bothered her greatly, and she began to pray for them. Every time we prayed, she prayed for the children of Ethiopia—mealtime, bedtime and any other time the thought came to her. She believed that her prayers made a difference in the lives of children halfway around the world. And, knowing the strength and passion of her faith, I am sure they did.

Our son David was a worrier from a very early age. He would be worried and anxious over things that *had* happened, that *could* happen, or that *might* or *might not* ever happen! To help him with this, one of the first scriptures we had him commit to memory was, in shortened form, "Don't worry about anything, but pray about everything. And the peace of God that transcends understanding will be yours" (Philippians 4:6–7).

Prayer is one of the greatest gifts God has given us, and it is one of the most precious gifts we can in turn give to our children. Prayer brings our children into the presence of God. When children learn to pray at a very early age, they learn that God is real, that he is strong and that he cares for them.

Pray with Your Children

Many parents pray with their children at bedtime and at meals, and while that is certainly a good thing, we need to teach our kids that prayer is much more than something we do at only certain times in the day. Prayer is a way we can go to God when we need help, when we are worried and when we are afraid.

I still remember the times as a young mother when everything seemed out of control—the children were fussing, and I was "losing it"—and I would say, "Stop everything! We need to pray." The kids and I would sit down, usually on the stairs that led into our kitchen, and we would take turns asking God to forgive us and to help us. I would pray to be a better mother, and they would ask to be better children. We would end our prayer and start over again, reminded that God was in our midst and that he heard and saw us, and would help us to do things differently.

I think those early prayers made God a very real and present part of our life then, and they have carried all of my children into adulthood. There are still many times even now that one of the kids will call and ask me to pray with them when they are worried, upset or about to face a challenging situation.

Pray by Yourself

Mothers, pray with your children, but also pray when you

are by yourself. Make the time to go to God when you are alone. You are doing the world's most important job, and you cannot do it on your own. You need God's strength, his guidance and his peace. Talking to God will keep *you* reminded that God is indeed God, and that he is able to do what you cannot.

Whatever else or however much you may have to do, take the time to pray. Get up a little earlier, stay up a little later. Pause for a moment during the busyness of the day. Pray during those quiet moments in the night when you are nursing a baby. You may not always have an extended time to pray, but do what you can. As a young mother I clung to the fact that Jesus said we would not be heard for our many words (Matthew 6:7).

Honestly, it is challenging to have lengthy, uninterrupted time with God during the time in life when we are raising young children. I think those were the years that taught me to "take God with me," to walk with him and to "pray continually." I called these short talks with God my "bullet prayers" because I fired them off rapidly. In this way I learned how to talk conversationally and naturally to him on and off throughout the day.

That being said, while I am glad I was forced to rely on God in this way, these short conversations alone were not enough to give me the closeness to God that I needed. Just as in any relationship, we still have to have some extended time to be truly close. In speaking to God in prayer, we all need time when we can really open up our heart and tell him all that is in it.

Sometimes we need time to sit still by ourselves and meditate on God and all that he has done in our lives and all that he wants to do in our lives right now.

We may need to get up earlier than our children, or we may need to take some time to pray while our children are napping. Of course, we mothers know that children seem to have a sixth sense about these times and will wake up earlier or in some other way not cooperate with our need for time alone with God. But I urge you, no matter what the obstacles, to keep on trying.

Mothers, it takes work to keep your relationship with God vibrant and strong during these years with young children. There will be times when you are driven to God out of need, but there are other times when life is just busy, and we may not rely on him as we need to. But we always need God, whether we "feel" like it or not and whether we think we have time for him or not. Whatever it takes, fight to be close to God.

In closing, never underestimate the power of a child's early prayer life to shape their future relationship with God. Our daughter Alexandra is now a young woman of strong faith, and it is my belief that much of the foundation of her faith was laid in her prayer life as a young child. She always prayed about the things on her heart, and she expected God to answer her prayers.

On one occasion, Sam and Alexandra decided to be "prayer partners," and each one committed to praying for one another about something special on each of their hearts. In a very short amount of time, their prayer for Sam was undeniably answered. He shared about his answered prayer one day in a sermon, and people began to ask Alexandra to pray for them! She took their requests seriously, and she always remembered to pray for them. Even today, Alexandra has an exceptional faith that her prayers will be answered and, indeed, they are.

Young mothers, pray with your children, pray by yourself, and always pray. Just as this was a practice that did not come easily to Jesus' disciples, it won't always be easy for us, but as the disciples asked of Jesus, so can we: "Lord, teach us to pray" (Luke 11:1).

BUILDING BLOCKS

☐ How do you need to grow in your prayer life? Do you need some consistent time alone with God? Then set aside some time today when you can pour out your heart to God. Do you need to pray more consistently throughout the day? Then concentrate on doing that today. Perhaps you need to bring prayer into your everyday life with your children. Then do so. Pray together when things begin to get chaotic, or when one of you is worried or anxious. Pray together when things are going well and everyone is happy! Make prayer a natural and real part of your life today—and every day.

☐ Philippians 4:6–7
Do not be anxious about anything, but in everything, by prayer and petition, with thanksgiving, present your requests to God. And the peace of God, which transcends all understanding, will guard your hearts and your minds in Christ Jesus.

Sisterhood of the Traveling Diapers

- Elizabeth -

Each heart knows its own bitterness,
and no one else can share its joy.

Proverbs 14:10

The Tender Years are rife with paradoxes. How can you constantly be surrounded by people—one smearing jelly on your hand, one tugging on your pant leg, another drooling on your shoulder—but still have no one to talk to?

How can you feel isolated when even your most intimate of moments—going to the bathroom—is a spectator sport, complete with commentary? ("Mommy, you're a big girl, you don't need anyone to help you wipe!") Everyone tells me that these years will fly by, but how can a rainy day at home alone with toddlers drag on for ages?

When you first become a mother, as awe-inspiring and joyous as the transformation is, it can still be a shock to adjust, in one cataclysmic day, from the total freedom of an unfettered woman, to feeling tethered to your house (and your baby!). And while you're nursing a baby—talk about the world's cutest little ball and chain!

Don't you sometimes think back on your carefree pre-baby days with awe? When we ran out of milk, we used to jump in the car and go buy some, without thinking twice about it. Getting out of the car required no forethought or strategy; we just...got out of the car!

When a friend called and asked us to see a movie, off we'd go! Now, it takes us fifteen minutes to load and unload the car, and having coffee with a friend requires planetary alignment and weeks of strategizing.

My grandmother had four girls in five years, but she speaks fondly of all the families in her neighborhood who helped her survive those years with her sanity intact. The men took the sole family car to work while the women stayed home with the kids. They formed a close-knit community of women and children who ran in and out of each other's homes all day long. With a few exceptions, most transient American neighborhoods don't work that way anymore. Even with more ways to communicate than ever before, many of us still feel isolated.

We're lucky to have the telephone, you say? I don't know about you, but at this point in my kids' lives, the phone is not much of a help—I can hardly hear, thanks to the constant flood of baby babbles, toddler demands and sibling rivalry screams in the background! At least now I can *text* my friends, so silence is not necessary to have a makeshift conversation.

As hard as we try to stay connected by spending time with other moms and kids, the forces of nature seem to conspire against us: illnesses, differing nap schedules, early bed times, grouchy kids...the list of deterrents goes on and on. I have learned the hard way that I should never tell Cassidy, my little social butterfly, where we are going until we are in the car, *and* I have confirmed with the other mother that she is also on her way!

Kevin and I have been trying for the past six weeks to

spend time with another family, but every week one of us has had a different sick child. I haven't been to a church service in about a month because every weekend one of my children has been sick. (Since Kevin is a minister, he can't miss service, so I always get Sunday sick duty.)

Last year, a group of four moms attempted to put together a weekly play group. Thanks to illnesses and schedule conflicts, we only managed to get together about four times in six months! Sound familiar? I know I'm not the only one who experiences these roadblocks to relationships—such frustrations are universal for young mothers.

It can be tempting to just give up and make our husband and kids our whole world. In many ways, they *are* and *should be* our whole world (in Titus 2:4–5 the Bible encourages young moms to "love their husbands and children...[and] to be busy at home")—but even so, we still need friendships. I try not to put all of my social needs on my husband. Sensitive as he is, he can only handle so many chick flicks, in-depth relationship psychoanalyses and fashion questions! I need other moms to both laugh and commiserate with and to compare notes on potty training and discipline dilemmas. I don't want to find, when my children have grown, that my life has become so consumed by theirs that I have lost all my own friends in the process.

Having friendships of our own takes creativity, perseverance, and lots of help from willing husbands, relatives and babysitters—but it is worth it. Preschools, library story times, Mommy and Me groups, Facebook, text messaging, girls' nights out—whatever it takes, keep up the friendships in your life, and keep loneliness at bay. And don't torture yourself unnecessarily by being a permanent slave to your kids' schedules: If someone has to miss a nap every once in a while so you can meet up with friends, sometimes it's worth it! I'm all about schedules and nap times and bedtimes, but my theory is that if I train my kids to be flexible while they're young, they'll learn to nap or sleep in different places on occasion, and I'll be a much happier mommy.

As I write this, my toddlers are playing at a Mother's Morning Out program, and my four-month-old is happily snoozing in her stroller while I write at Barnes and Noble, surrounded by all my bookstore buddies who see me here twice a week!

But as much as I encourage you to try to nurture your friendships, I have had to surrender to my life as it is right now—and you will need to do the same, if you haven't already. I spent three years pleading with God to give me this family—and I never, ever want to be ungrateful for the precious bedlam that keeps me home.

On days when we have no plans, or someone is sick and we are home-bound, I have learned to keep company with God throughout the day. Sometimes I roll my eyes to heaven, knowing that God is laughing with me at my kids' shenanigans. Or, when I feel completely stumped and overwhelmed, I just beg him, over and over again, "Help, help, help, help," because I don't even know what *kind* of help I need!

The fact is that while we have babies and preschool-age kids (especially during the winter months when someone is sick at all times), it is going to be difficult for us to have lots of times with our girlfriends. Sure, we should take advantage of every opportunity we can, but we are not total losers if we feel a bit lonely from time to time. It's not healthy or fair for us to compare our lives and friendships now to what they were like in college, when we were a bunch of single girls with no responsibilities, running around town and having spontaneous slumber parties!

After Cassidy was born, I felt frustrated that I couldn't seem to get close to anyone new. We had only lived in Athens for a few years, and since infertility struggles had put us a few years behind our peers in the child-rearing game, I felt isolated. Since then, I've worked hard to draw closer to some other young moms, but at the same time I have come to peace with my friendships, and I feel content and confident.

I've realized that friendships are what they are. We cannot *make* someone our best friend. Friendship, like love, is one of those mysterious chemistry things. That magical "best friend" who *gets* you and adores you and finishes your thoughts is a rare gift from God that might come along once or twice *in a lifetime*—maybe a few more, if you're really fortunate.

I am not a member of a Ya-Ya Sisterhood or a Sisterhood of the Traveling Pants, but I am doing my best to build my own circle of friends—we'll call it the Sisterhood of the Traveling Diapers. I am learning not to compare one friendship to another or to have unrealistic expectations, but just to appreciate each relationship for what it is, without trying to force them all into the same mold.

If we open our hearts, we can enjoy a great variety of friendships, each with its own unique blessings. Some are "mommy" friends: Our children are the same ages, so they play together while we spend most of our time comparing notes on kid stuff. Others are "deep talk" friends: We love talking about life and spiritual issues, and we try to help each other grow. Still others are "hobby" friends: We share the same interests, so we always have fun together. And then there are the truly rare finds: our "hubby" friends, whose husbands also hit it off well with ours. I feel especially fortunate to have a lot of "younger sister" friends—students in my husband's campus ministry who come over to spend time with me and my kids.

I feel lavishly blessed with a number of fulfilling, lifetime friendships. But even so, my husband is still my best friend—as he should be. God is my only perfect friend—and always will be. My daughters, my little buddies-in-training, are precious future friendships—at least, I pray they will be. But in the meantime, my life is rich, my heart is full, and my minivan is on the move.

BUILDING BLOCKS

☐ This week, be the friend you wish you had. Call someone just to say hi, or drop a card in the mail. Thoughtfulness has a way of coming back around!

☐ Galatians 6:2
Carry each other's burdens, and in this way you will fulfill the law of Christ.

First Dance

Elizabeth Laing Thompson

A dimpled finger points; impatient grunts plead:
Music, Mommy.
Laughing, I turn on his favorite.
Bobbing and swaying side to side; part robot, part rooster,
he dances.
My little Frankenstein.
Eyes bright with mischief, cheeks flushed with joy,
he wraps sticky fingers around mine and pulls me in:
Dance with me, Mommy.
We dance,
squealing and giggling, until he hiccups and I stagger into the kitchen table.
Breathless, I flash forward.

> A young man, tall and dark-haired and dashing in a tuxedo,
>   just like his father.
> His hand beckons:
> *Dance with me, Mom.*
> The smiling crowd parts for me.
> Those same twinkling eyes draw me in, still with their secret joke.
> His hand—manly and strong and sticky with icing—swallows mine.
> We dance.
> Graceful, athletic, he sweeps me in a circle until the crowd blurs;
> twirling, remembering, we wipe tears from our eyes.
> Mostly my eyes.
> I flash back to a dance with a nearly-two-year-old,
> the memory so thick I cannot breathe.
> We float past a white wisp—
> a beautiful young woman, waiting her turn.
> And now it will always be her turn.
> The music fades, he kisses my cheek,
> my hand lingers on his, and I pass the torch.

Eyes clouded with tears,
I sweep him up into my arms,
spin him around and smother him with kisses until he squirms:
Let me go, Mommy.

I will. But not today.

It Takes a Village

- Geri -

Two are better than one,
> because they have a good return for their work:

If one falls down,
> his friend can help him up.

But pity the man who falls
> and has no one to help him up!

Ecclesiastes 4:9–10

We cannot accomplish the daunting task of raising children without the help and the influence of other people. We need other women to teach us how to be mothers, and our children need people *besides* their mothers in their lives! This is God's plan—it was never his intention that we would be independent from others. In fact, it was always God's idea that we would be a part of something bigger than ourselves.

The thing is, most of us do have people we can learn from and who can give us needed support, but all too often we don't value their importance, and may not even recognize who they are. Let's take a few minutes to think about some of these people.

Older Women

The Bible specifically talks about the importance of learning from women who are older than we are. Paul tells us that the older women in the church should "...train the younger women to love their husbands and children, to be self-controlled and pure, to be busy at home, to be kind and to be subject to their husbands" (Titus 2:4–5).

There is nothing like learning from someone who has already "been there, done that." The mother of older or grown children has a perspective that you cannot yet have when you are right in the middle of raising your own kids. The old saying that "hindsight is 20/20" is in many ways true. When you have already gone through the challenges of rearing children, you have the perspective of looking back and seeing what did and didn't work, and what did and didn't matter.

We can learn valuable lessons from those who have experienced failure and made mistakes. An older woman doesn't have to have done it perfectly to be able to help a young mother. In her humility she can admit mistakes and perhaps help a young mother to avoid them. Who knows how much heartbreak could be prevented if young women would learn from those mothers and wives who have gone before them.

There is a unique bond of compassion and empathy that connects all mothers regardless of their ages. A mother is always a mother, whether her children are young or are grown with children of their own. I have seen this in the relationship that Elizabeth has with her grandmother (my mother), a relationship which has grown even closer over the past several years. My mother had four children born close together; in fact, her first three children were spaced exactly as Elizabeth's three children are (fourteen months between the first two and then just twenty months between the second and third children). This shared experience gives my mother a special understanding of Elizabeth's life right now. She remembers, she understands...and she somehow survived!

The definition of "older" is different for all of us—especially as you get older yourself. After all, we are all older—and younger—than somebody. But whatever our situation, we need women of various ages in our lives. We need the influence of those who are quite a few years older than we, who have progressed all the way through the years of raising children. And we need to be close to some women who are only a few steps ahead of us in life. Learn from these women. Watch them, listen to them, and let them into your heart and your life.

Young Mothers

We also need the friendship and support of other young mothers—our peers, those who can walk hand in hand with us on the journey. There is nothing more rewarding than the special camaraderie that comes from sharing the ups and downs of raising children. These are some of the relationships that will sustain you when your children are small and will still be there long after the kids are grown and gone.

When I think of this kind of friendship, I always think of my friend Jane. We became friends in Atlanta when our children were very young. Every week we took our combined brood of six small children, all preschoolers, to McDonald's so we could spend time together. We brought books, puzzles and games (this was before the days of the incredible in-store playgrounds), and ordered pancakes for the children. While they ate and played, we drank coffee and enjoyed being together. Even though our children are now grown, Jane and I are still close friends, navigating new stages of life together, and now planning time to take our grandchildren to McDonald's together.

As much as women need friendships, we can sometimes find ourselves estranged and lonely. I think there are two weaknesses we have that contribute to this. First, we compare ourselves unfavorably to other mothers, and second, we become competitive with one another. We compare our husbands, marriages, houses, appearance and even our children. Instead of learning from and valuing the different strengths we each have, we become insecure. Instead of being happy for a friend's accomplishments, we become jealous. What could be friendships that grow closer and deeper with time are driven apart by insecurity and misunderstanding.

Do you want to develop meaningful friendships with other women? Then genuinely share one another's joys, fears and burdens. Help one another emotionally. Serve each other. Be yourself. Be open. Be vulnerable.

Learn from one another's strengths. Each of us has unique strengths as mothers. Some of you find it easy to be warm and affectionate with your children. Others of you know how to talk with your kids in a way that fosters heartfelt communication. Some of you know how to relax and have fun with them; you haven't forgotten how to play. Others excel at balancing work and family, or at running a household and organizing a home.

Instead of feeling like a failure because some of these are not your strengths, appreciate them in others. Observe them, ask questions, and learn. You may never be as strong as another woman in some areas, but you can learn and grow. And *you* can help other mothers in your areas of strength.

Your Husband

It takes a lot of people to help us raise our children, and none is more important than your husband. Learn to work as a team and not against or independent of one another. You are in this thing together. Instead of criticizing each other's differences, help each other. Together your individual strengths and weaknesses combine to make a very effective parent!

The Church

It does take a village to raise our children, and I cannot think of the village without thinking about the church. The church was one of the most important parts of my children's lives as they were growing up. They have wonderful memories of Sunday school teachers, church friends and warm fellowship. When Elizabeth was about three years old, she was so at home at church, that she would go up to everyone asking them for chewing gum. When we learned about this, we spoke with her, telling her that it was bad manners to go around church asking for gum. We let her know she could only have chewing gum if people offered it to her.

Next thing we knew, she was going up to people with the ingenious request, "Would you please *offer me* some gum?" Needless to say, she felt very comfortable in the fellowship and loved being at church. I will always be thankful for all of the Christians who loved our children and were such an important part of their lives. These were the people they admired, loved and wanted to grow up to be like.

Teachers and Babysitters

There are so many others in this village of life; the list goes on and on. I think admiringly of our children's teachers. I encourage you to make them your friends and advisers, not your adversaries! They see your children in settings that you do not, and they can be an invaluable source of help and influence.

I am also reminded of our kids' babysitters. Choose them wisely, and realize the great influence and example they can be. I still remember Eleanor and Evelyn, my own favorite babysitters when I was a little girl. They were fun and caring, and set a great example of what I wanted to be like when I grew up!

&

It does take a village to raise a child. Regardless of how you may sometimes feel, you are not in this alone! You have many people who love you and your children, and who want to help. Open your heart and let them in. You will be a wiser and better mother because of their influence.

Ultimately, you and their dad are the ones responsible for raising your kids (unless, of course, you are a single mom). Watch, learn, listen and pray. With God's help and wisdom— and with all the good people he has put in your life, you are going to do just fine!

BUILDING BLOCKS

☐ Make one phone call today. If you need some wisdom or guidance, call an older woman and ask her advice. If you need companionship and a friend, call another young mother. If you know of a younger mom who just had her first baby, reach out to her and give her a call of encouragement.

☐ Ephesians 4:14–16
Then we will no longer be infants, tossed back and forth by the waves, and blown here and there by every wind of teaching and by the cunning and craftiness of men in their deceitful scheming. Instead, speaking the truth in love, we will in all things grow up into him who is the

Head, that is, Christ. From him the whole body, joined and held together by every supporting ligament, grows and builds itself up in love, as each part does its work.

Still the One

– Geri –

The Lord God said, "It is not good for man to be alone. I will make a helper suitable for him."

Genesis 2:18

I loved the years Sam and I spent raising our four children. They were busy, exhausting years filled with fun, laughter and good times. They were also amazing years because I watched as four tiny infants grew into the incredible young men and women they are today. I still look at my children and marvel at the transformation that unfolded before my eyes, and I am thankful that I was a part of something so wonderful.

But how sad it would be if that were the end! I loved the years we spent raising our children. I love the relationships we have now that they are adults. I love being a grandmother. But there is something even greater that I am thankful for: I still love my husband, and I love the life we have together even after the children have gone.

During the years that Sam was a campus minister, one of the saddest things he dealt with were the calls from college students whose parents had decided to divorce. After years of raising children, they found themselves alone in a house empty not only of children, but of the love they once shared with each other. After the kids moved away, there was nothing left to hold the marriage together. What should have marked a new beginning in their life instead became the end.

Next to faith in God, the greatest gift you can give to your children will be the lifelong example of a loving and devoted marriage relationship. When they see you as a united front, when they see genuine warmth and affection between Mom and Dad, they can be secure. God's plan is that marriage lasts a lifetime, and that it not only lasts, but grows in love, fulfillment and companionship. It is the one relationship that outshines and outlasts all others; it is "until death do us part."

It is not easy to keep a warm, vibrant marriage during some of the stressful years of raising a family. It takes a conscious decision followed up with concentrated time and effort to keep your marriage strong. Our energies and our thoughts can become so consumed with the needs of our children, running a household, and earning a living that we neglect each other. We can become more like business partners or roommates than lovers and best friends. In time, we drift apart, held together only by all the things that must be done rather than by a warm, loving relationship.

There were a number of times when Sam and I had to sit down with one another, take stock and recommit to making our marriage special and close. These times of renewal usually took place after the addition of another child into our family. The biggest adjustment we made in our marriage was after our first child was born. Honestly, I was not prepared for how all-consuming a mother's love could be. I became so focused on my newborn child, Elizabeth, that I neglected my husband. I lost desire sexually and generally treated Sam as a roommate rather than a lover.

I remember the talks we had and the tears we shed. Above all I remember the decision that I made: He and our marriage would come first in my heart regardless of how tired I was, or even the current state of my emotions. That was the most important decision I have made since the day I said "I do." And, it was one I made over and over again as I went through the continuing cycles of childbirth, nursing and raising small children.

As I look back upon it today, I realize that this decision not only saved my marriage, but my soul, and probably the souls of my children as well. We actually laugh about it now. I used to try to explain to Sam that all of the cuddling a mother gives to her baby can diminish her desire for sexual intimacy with her husband. Sam would look at me with an incredulous look on his face and say: "I have held and cuddled the children. I talk to other fathers who hold and cuddle their children. Let me assure you; there is not a man alive who can relate to what you just said!"

As our family grew larger, we continued to make additional adjustments to keep our marriage strong. After David was born, we decided to get a babysitter on Saturday mornings so we could go out to breakfast for some uninterrupted time together.

After Jonathan was born, I remember having some more of those tearful talks about the need for us to stay close emotionally and romantically even though we were exhausted so much of the time.

When Alexandra was born, life became even busier, and we had to work to make our time together about us and our love for one another, and not just about the kids' needs and running a household.

We did this by focusing on simple things such as showing affection and taking the time to talk during the day. We made time to go to dinner or out by ourselves, or to get away for a night or two at a bed and breakfast. We made up our minds to keep a tone of love and respect in the way we spoke to one another. We strove to continue to grow in our marriage even while we were busy trying to grow in our parenting.

Looking back after all these years, I can say that the investment we made in our marriage was more than worth it! Young mothers, let me encourage you to nurture your marriage all along the way. Care for it, devote yourself to it. Your marriage will truly be a well-spring of love and companionship long after the children are grown and gone. You will miss your children when they go out to build their own lives, and you will forever treasure the memories of those precious days and years with them. But you will love that special time in your life when, once again, you have a quiet house and you have each other to love and to enjoy for the rest of your days.

BUILDING BLOCKS

☐ What can you do *today* that will encourage your husband? It may be something as simple as being more affectionate, fixing his favorite dinner or writing him a card. Do something to let him know that he is special and loved by you.

☐ Proverbs 31:10–12
  A wife of noble character who can find?
    She is worth far more than rubies.
  Her husband has full confidence in her
    and lacks nothing of value.
  She brings him good, not harm,
    all the days of her life.

Wife First, Mommy Second

– Elizabeth –

May your fountain be blessed,
and may you rejoice in the wife of your youth.

Proverbs 5:18

I still get chills when I hear my children's Minnie Mouse voices call me that most prestigious of titles: *Mommy*. At last—at long, long last—I am a Mommy. I spent almost three years doubting whether I would ever bear my husband children. I pleaded with God to let me see what our combined love (and DNA!) would look like in human form—would a son inherit my hazel eyes and Kevin's quarterback shoulders? Would a daughter get his thick black hair and my unruly cowlicks?

Now when I look at my children's little round faces, I gaze in wonder. Here before me, crawling and giggling and destroying things, lives the precious proof of my love for my husband, and his for me. God has granted us the unfathomable gift of bearing our own children, the product of our passion and commitment to one another.

How is it then, that children borne out of a loving marriage can so easily, so quickly knock the marriage from its place of utmost importance? How can we forget to nurture the relationship—and even the process—that produced a baby in the first place? Sometime during the beached-whale last weeks of pregnancy and the zombie-making first months with a newborn, a shift can take place—a change that should be only temporary, but that some couples never reverse: Our children become our first priority. We even brag about putting our kids first, as if that were a good thing!

First the baby takes over our body—in one way when we are pregnant, and then in different ways after they are born. (If you have nursed a baby, you may be familiar with the look of envy on your husband's face as he watches the newborn "borrowing" his favorite body part!) But the takeover doesn't stop with our bodies. From the moment children enter the world, screaming the news of their arrival, they dominate our time, snatch our sleep and shrink our sex drive—and somewhere along the way, they also steal our hearts.

Of course, that's not all bad! To some extent, it's a normal part of raising and adoring our children. Many of the sacrifices we make for our kids are good and necessary ones—but even so, we must preserve the sanctity and priority of our marriage. And that takes work! Even if you've always had an "easy" marriage, a close relationship during the Tender Years will not just happen. It will take deliberate effort and attention.

After our initial struggles to conceive, I have now been either pregnant or nursing for four straight years. (Yes, we did it on purpose, and yes, we are crazy.) Blessed as we feel, we are battling to maintain our friendship and romance amidst all the chaos. It is not easy to stay close when we can hardly have a single uninterrupted conversation all day. Forget lingering over a candlelit meal—our family dinners are often laughable affairs. I wolf my food as fast as possible, hoping to get a full meal in before someone melts down.

Let me share three magic words that will save your marriage during these tornadic years: *Get a babysitter!* As often as you can manage it—maybe once a week or every other week—spend some time alone with your husband, away from the kids.

Some young moms are convinced that they are the only people in the world who can keep their children safe. Some will not trust their kids with anyone except *maybe* their own mother—and even then, they nearly hyperventilate when they walk out of the door.

Come on, my control-freak friend, give yourself a break! Of course no one can care for your children the way you can, but other women do know a thing or two about childcare, and they may even do some things better than you! Most children are not that fragile.

Think about it: Our kids are far more likely to get injured while in *our* care than in someone else's, as other people will likely be much *more* paranoid about their safety than we are. I promise, leaving your children with a trustworthy babysitter so you can go out for a few hours with your husband is not going to scar your kids' psyches! But a distant, neglected, loveless marriage—now *that* will do some harm.

Even if your kids cry for a minute when you leave, they will be fine and will probably begin laughing and playing within minutes. I have found that my kids often have *more* fun with babysitters than with me because a babysitter can give them their undivided attention (whereas I also have to be concerned about cleaning my house and doing the laundry), and a babysitter brings fresh ideas for play.

The earlier that you get into the practice of leaving your kids for brief periods, the more flexible they will be, and the less painful the separation will be (for you and for your kids!). Take advantage of their malleability as infants, and teach them that the world does not end just because Mommy is not holding them for an hour or two.

By the time all of our babies were a month old, we left them with a sitter for a little while so we could go out to lunch. After a few more weeks, we even got brave enough to try a movie. The first few times, we always stayed close to home, in case of an emergency, but we've never yet had to rescue a baby from a babysitter!

When I was pregnant with Cassidy, a good friend gave me the best practical advice I've ever received. Knowing that I planned to breastfeed the baby, she suggested that I pump milk and get the baby to take a bottle by the time she was three weeks old. And so, with all three kids, I have made sure to offer them a bottle by the time they were three or four weeks old, when nursing was well established, but they were still flexible enough to accept something new. As a result, all three of my kids have nursed beautifully but have also been happy to drink bottles on occasion, so I have not been permanently chained to them. This has enabled Kevin and me to resume going on dates fairly soon after each baby was born—with the added benefit that nursing has not been an overwhelming social and marital burden. (Thank you, Allison!)

I will never forget how happy Kevin was the first time he took me on a date after our third child, Avery, was born. We dropped all three kids off with my brave in-laws, and when we got back into the gloriously empty and quiet van, Kevin nearly sang, "I'm going to hang out with my best friend!" I laughed and warmed all over, caught off guard by how excited he was to have me all to himself.

I'd been so busy taking care of the kids that I hadn't realized how much he was missing time alone with me. Of course, I had missed him too, but I just hadn't had any time to register it!

We mothers can be so busy taking care of the kids, so ful-filled in our life as a Mommy, that we don't notice that our husband is missing us and needing us. And unlike our kids, who have no problem making demands, our husbands will probably not tell us that they are feeling lonely or neglected.

And it's not just women who can be guilty of giving our children too much attention. When Cassidy was about five months old, cooing and smiling at everything that moved, I remember feeling a little hurt that when Kevin would come home, his eyes would first land on Cassidy instead of me—his greeting to me felt like an afterthought. We *both* needed time alone together to renew our relationship.

I can hear some of you now: "But we can't afford a babysit-ter!" If you are not fortunate enough to have parents nearby, who will practically pay *you* to let them keep your kids, then the cost of babysitting can be intimidating. But I look at it as an investment in my marriage. I can think of nothing I'd rather spend money on than preserving a close relationship with my husband! So if having coffee with Kevin costs us $5 for coffee ($1 for Kevin; $4 for me—unfortunately, I like the expensive ones) and $20 for babysitting—well, it will be the most meaningful $25 cup of coffee we've ever had!

Sometimes, because babysitting is so expensive, we spend all our date money to pay the sitter, then find some-thing free to do together. Remember your broke dating days, when you had to be creative if you wanted to go out? Play tennis, hike, take a picnic to a park, window shop, star gaze... We have countless free options, and they are often more bonding and romantic than staring side-by-side at a movie screen!

And try some out-of-the-box solutions to the babysitting dilemma. Some families take turns babysitting: One couple keeps all the kids one Friday night while the other parents go out; then they swap roles the next weekend. Our gym offers patrons a date night on Fridays—you can leave your kids in the gym nursery for a couple of hours while you go out to dinner.

However you finagle it, make time for your marriage. One hour connecting over lunch now could save hours of "discussion" later; a few babysitting dollars now could save thousands in therapy dollars later! Show your children how valuable your husband is to you. One day, they will thank you.

BUILDING BLOCKS

☐ Take a look at this month's calendar, and plan a time to go out with your man. Breakfast, coffee, dinner, a movie, even a long walk... It doesn't matter what you do together, as long as *together* does not include your progeny!

☐ Song of Songs 5:16
His mouth is sweetness itself;
    he is altogether lovely.
This is my lover, this is my friend,
    O daughters of Jerusalem.

Got Romance?

- Elizabeth -

Place me like a seal over your heart,
   like a seal on your arm;
for love is as strong as death,
   its jealousy unyielding as the grave.
It burns like blazing fire,
   like a mighty flame.
Many waters cannot quench love;
   rivers cannot wash it away.
If one were to give
   all the wealth of his house for love,
   it would be utterly scorned.

Song of Songs 8:6–7

Sex. It does a marriage good.

(Yes, I'd like to thank the dairy industry for the advertising campaigns that provided inspiration for this chapter.)

How quickly a new baby can torpedo our romantic lives! We who once delighted in making whoopee now think, "Big whoop." We who once wore cute negligees to bed to woo our husband now don his old boxers and stained T-shirts, because they fit our new extra-large shape, and they're the only clothes we can find that are clean. We who once enjoyed romantic evenings with our man, who didn't mind staying up a little later to spend time with him, now fall asleep standing in the shower. We are like the woman in Song of Songs (I bet that she, too, was an overworked young mother): "You are a garden locked up, my sister, my bride, you are a spring enclosed, a sealed fountain" (4:12). Sound familiar? Our holey T-shirt and boxer shorts scream: "Closed for business. Keep out!"

And it's not just the wives who are rarely "in the mood"; our husbands are often just as tired as we are! By the time Kevin and I get all three kids in bed—sometimes a major, emotionally draining battle, as you can read in other chapters—and then clean up the kitchen and put in a load of laundry, it's 9:30, and we are catatonic with exhaustion. Forget sex—we just want to sleep!

Want two words that will keep your marriage vibrant and close? *Make love!* Even if you don't want to. Even if you are terrified of leaking milk all over the place. Even if you smell like spit-up. Even if you have forgotten what "in the mood" feels like. Even if you still have some extra squish, and you feel as sexy as cold oatmeal. Even if you haven't had time to shave your legs. For three weeks. Just jump on your husband, and see if you don't have a good time and feel reconnected.

Last weekend, I was in tears because I didn't feel close to my husband. Because of various illnesses, it had been a little over a week since our last interlude, and I was *not* in the mood. But Sunday night...*ahem*...and you know what? I was shocked to find that all my feelings of distance vanished. After ten years of marriage, I re-learned an old lesson: When I don't feel close, it might be that we are not communicating; it could be that we haven't had enough time together; it might be that he hasn't brought flowers in a while—but it could be that we just need to have sex. That simple! And it doesn't even have to be a lingering, candlelit extravaganza. Fifteen minutes might do the trick! How's that for a magic marriage pill? Perhaps, while our children are young, we should take Solomon's advice in Song of Songs 1:4: "Take me away with you—let us hurry!"

But as you know, even fifteen minutes can be hard to come by when you have little ones! My mom has told me that she used to strap me into a high chair with some Cheerios and *Sesame Street*, and run into the bedroom with my dad for a few minutes. (I know, it's a little weird when it's your parents, but having heard my parents speak about marriage for so many years—well, I'm over it now!)

The sad reality is that, while our children are young, we sometimes have to schedule in time for romance. Kevin often works at night, so it helps us, at the beginning of the week, to discuss which nights we will both try to shut life down a little earlier, so we can—er—"sleep" together, before we sleep together. Kevin initially resisted my pleas to schedule romance, preferring to have things happen spontaneously. But for now, reality is trumping spontaneity. Not to say that we never have unexpected romps together, but Kevin has finally realized that, if we are to maintain any sort of consistent romantic life—and especially if he wants me to have any sort of energy or interest in the proposition—we are going to have to plan ahead a little. I need fair warning, so I can switch my brain from baby mama to hot mama. Plus, I need to plan ahead if I'm going to wash all the spit-up off my shoulders!

My next suggestion may rock your world if you have a new baby: As soon as you are able to get away for an overnight tryst with your husband, do it! I'm serious! It feels so strange to leave your child overnight for the first time, but it will do wonders for your marriage, not to mention your sanity.

We have managed to leave each of our babies for a night when they were about six months old. I realize that some readers may be ready to pass out with shock, but hang with me! We waited until they were sleeping well through the night (please don't hate me—I know my babies accomplished this most blessed feat a bit early), and enlisted the prodigious babysitting skills of my intrepid in-laws. Every time, I was still nursing, so I pumped and froze milk ahead of time, and took a breast pump with me to the hotel (really sexy, I know).

I cried and felt panicky when we first left, but within a short time, I relaxed and began to enjoy myself. And the babies did beautifully! They hardly even noticed my absence, since they were asleep for most of the time, and the brief separation did not damage my connection with them or their attachment to me.

Even now, I am so thankful that Kevin and I had those little breaks from parenting. In a short time, we were able to reconnect and breathe, to spend time together without feeling "on the clock." We got a really good night's sleep—although sleep wasn't high on our priority list! We remembered what it was like to be married, not just to be parents, and we made memories that were just us, not us and the babies.

When we returned home the next day, we felt close, invigorated and more excited than ever to see our children again. We are still on a high from our most recent escapade just weeks ago, when we celebrated our tenth anniversary and marveled at the blessings of the past ten years.

So what are you waiting for? If you have the time to read this book, then your children are probably asleep—so put down the book and run find your husband! Or call him at work and tell him, in the words of that memorable country song, that he "left something turned on at home...."

BUILDING BLOCKS

☐ Once this week, test out the fifteen-minute tumble. See, now, don't you feel better? Think through your schedule and consider what night or nights each week are ideal for you and your husband to spend extra time together. Ask him if you can rendezvous in the bedroom a little early those nights. Be prepared to catch him when he faints.

☐ Genesis 2:18
The LORD God said, "It is not good for the man to be alone."

You Are Special

– Geri –

Our children need to know that they are special, that they are loved, and that each one has a place in our hearts which no one else has. Our example of loving in this manner is God himself. God loves the world—yes—but he loves each person in the world. He loves *me*—as a person, as an individual! He imagined me, made me, formed me, knew me and loved me even before I was born.

> For you created my inmost being;
>> you knit me together in my mother's womb.
> I praise you because I am fearfully and wonderfully made;
>> your works are wonderful,
>> I know that full well.
> My frame was not hidden from you
>> when I was made in the secret place.
> When I was woven together in the depths of the earth,
>> your eyes saw my unformed body. (Psalm 139:13–15)

Many of us struggle all of our lives to understand how special we are in the eyes of God. Knowing this was difficult to grasp, Paul prayed that we would be able to comprehend it:

> And I pray that you, being rooted and established in love, may have power, together with all the saints, to grasp how wide and long and high and deep is the love of Christ, and to know this love that surpasses knowledge— that you may be filled to the measure of all the fullness of God. (Ephesians 3:17–19)

God loves you, he likes you and he cares about everything in your life. He cries with you, and I believe he even laughs with you. He is always on your side—even when he disciplines you. He does not stop loving you, and he never forgets those things he likes about you. In the midst of the sea of humanity, he very personally knows *you* and cares about *you*. He gave you unique talents and abilities. He knows the number of hairs on your head—and even whether they are your natural color or not (Matthew 10:30). Mind-boggling, isn't it?

One of the ways we can come to better understand God's perfect and personal love is by contemplating the special love that we as mothers have for each of our children. No matter how many children we may have, each one is special to us.

Think about what makes each one of your children unique. Think deeply of the things you love about each of them. They each have their strengths and weaknesses—and to a mother, their weaknesses only make them more lovable! Give each child a place of love and esteem that is their own. In one sense, I do love each one of my four children "the most." Each of them has a place in my heart that no one else will ever be able to fill, a place that is theirs and theirs alone.

I saw this quite clearly when David was still very young. He was not quite two years old when our son Jonathan was born, and he had a difficult time adjusting. He became very emotional and difficult to handle. Nothing made him happy and everything was a fight.

One day, not knowing what else to do, I held him on my lap and started talking to him. He was still so little that I had no idea how much he was able to understand, but I talked anyway. I told him how much Daddy and I loved him, that we loved him in a way that we could never love anyone else. Yes, there was a new baby in our home, and we loved him very much, but that did not change in any way how much we loved David. He was a special little boy and no one would ever have his place in our hearts. There never would be another David. I told him that I wanted him to be happy and to know how very much God loved him and how much I loved him.

As I said, I honestly wasn't sure how much he could understand, but I can tell you this: Something inside him changed that day! He sat quietly as I talked, and then lay down calmly for his nap; he was a different child when he got up. It was one of those amazing moments God gives mothers, when you know in your heart that something special has happened. He from that time on understood that he was loved in a way that only he could ever be loved. To this day, I cherish the memory of that beautiful, private, once-in-a-lifetime moment with my son.

As with many aspects of motherhood, this concept is easy to appreciate, but difficult to put into practice. You may have one child to whom you easily relate and another who knows exactly how to "push your buttons." You may have one who is easy to talk to and another who clams up. When I taught preschool, there would always be some children in class that I found more difficult to like. I thought, *Yes, but these are someone else's kids. I'll never feel this way about my own children.*

Then I became a mother myself! I hate to admit it, but there were times in raising my own children when each of them was not very likeable. I felt terrible! *What kind of a mother am I?* I turned to God and learned to ask for his help. I knew that if my love was lacking or weak, his was not. I would pray something like this: *God, I know that you know this child; you made him (or her) and you like him (or her). Please open my eyes and help me see the things in him (or her) that are special and that you love.* I don't ever remember a time when God did not answer that prayer.

Each of your children is a unique soul—fashioned by the Creator himself. Learn to love and appreciate the special things about each one of them. And remember, God made each of your children just the way he wanted, and when he was done, he looked upon his creation and said "It is very good"—and then he broke the mold!

BUILDING BLOCKS

☐ Take some time today to think about each one of your children. What is special and unique about each of them? What are their talents and strengths, and how do those enrich you and the rest of your family? Now share this with them!

☐ Jeremiah 1:5
Before I formed you in the womb I knew you, before you were born I set you apart.

The Happy House

- Elizabeth -

Better a dry crust with peace and quiet
   than a house full of feasting, with strife.

Proverbs 17:1

Better to live on a corner of the roof
   than share a house with a quarrelsome wife.

Proverbs 21:9

When I think back on my childhood, I don't remember specific events so much as an overarching feeling: a love-drenched blend of serenity, simplicity, security. I am deeply thankful that those are the emotions I associate with growing up; I realize I am one of the fortunate few.

With four children in the Laing family, a sense of joy and harmony did not come naturally: It was the product of my parents' relentless focus, consistent discipline and pervasive spirituality. My father set a tone of godliness and expressiveness; my mother radiated joy and compassion. All four of us remember Mom's smile as just about our favorite thing in the world to see. And a bear hug from Dad could always right my topsy-turvy world.

In the first weeks of my marriage, I realized that *my* mood was going to dominate our entire home—for better or worse. I married a delightfully happy man who goes around the house whistling all the time, who thanks God at the end of *every* day for a "wonderful day"—and genuinely means it each time. I do not share Kevin's natural optimism and joy—I'm a bit more introspective and more easily upset. If something bothers me, I tend to hang on to it and analyze it inside and out for hours or even days.

In my younger years, I would give in to what my family called "funks"—I'd allow myself to wallow in guilt, worry or sadness for long periods of time. The first few times that I gave into funks as a newlywed, I saw a change in my upbeat husband: He seemed sad and overwhelmed and confused.

I quickly realized that I had to mature emotionally and to become unselfish in my moods if I wanted to have a happy family life in my new home, not to mention a happy husband. My mother wasn't there to cheer everyone up—that was *my* job now!

Since then, I have worked very hard to become a more positive, joyful, selfless person; to work out my concerns in prayer, and then leave them there with God. Kevin and I had a joke in the early days that would remind me to let go of my worries: When we'd pull into our driveway, he'd point to our house and say, "Do you see that house? That is the Happy House. Only happy people get to go inside that house!" Sounds silly, and it was, but it helped me, in a lighthearted way, to realize that I could put boundaries on my emotions.

Now that I have children, I am re-learning the same lessons, but in a different way. First, I am realizing that my children's behavior and attitudes cannot dictate my feelings or my confidence. If I base my emotional state on the whims of a baby and two toddlers, I'm in for a wacky ride!

On days when I let the battles get to me, I am not a fun wife for my husband when he comes home for dinner. I want our home and marriage to be his refuge from the world—not a place he longs to escape every morning!

In dealing with my own children, I am drawing a great deal on my parents' example in our home. Mom and Dad refused to allow one child's bad attitude to ruin life for the rest of the family. You know the kid I'm talking about: Everyone else is happy with their chicken, but Miss Pouty Pants wants spaghetti; the whole family agrees on a DVD to watch, but Mr. Opinionated insists on a different movie; everyone is laughing and having a good time, but Princess Sourpuss is in a bad mood and wants to bring the whole ship down with her. Ecclesiastes 9:18 says that "one sinner destroys much good." How true that is! It only takes one sour, selfish kid who is whining and fuming to spoil everyone else's day.

One of my parents' solutions was to remove the Stinker from the family. If someone chose to have a negative attitude, they could go have it all alone in their room—there they could sulk and moan to their heart's content, while the rest of us laughed and enjoyed life together.

This method usually had an amazing effect: The Stinker, facing a meal or an evening alone, with no audience for his or her Oscar-worthy dramatizations, would quickly repent and come out a happy and cooperative family member. Meanwhile, the rest of us continued enjoying ourselves, unscathed by the whims of the recalcitrant sibling. That is not to imply that my parents did not deal with our bad attitudes—quite the contrary!—but this plan of action often worked wonders.

I have begun employing this method already with Blake (age two) and Cassidy (age three), and it is proving effective. Cassidy still has limited control over her emotions, and the smallest things—an uncooperative zipper, a dirty nightgown—are catastrophic on her emotional Richter scale. She immediately throws herself to the ground, sobbing. I cannot reason with her when she is like that, and strong discipline sometimes backfires. Engaging with her often makes things worse, and somehow validates her tantrum.

In those moments, I find that if I calmly send her to her room and tell her to have her fit there and come out when she's happy again, she pulls herself together more quickly. And then there are the days when, for no apparent reason, she wakes up not just on the wrong side of the bed, but on the wrong side of town! She complains and whines from the moment she opens her eyes, until my nerves are fraying and I'm ready to lose it. On those days, I send her to her room and tell her to start the day over—to come out when she is ready to be pleasant. It doesn't work every time, but it often does help.

Just this morning, Cassidy was having a whiny moment, when she suddenly stopped in the middle of our discussion and said, "Can I start over?" Then she gave me a winning smile, and we backtracked and began our conversation all over again! In my heart, I celebrated a monumental parenting victory, after months of work. Just as I learned through my Happy House lesson, Cassidy is learning to put some boundaries on her outbursts.

When I recount stories to my mother about my kids, she will often give me subtle reminders that I am in charge, that I can set whatever mood I want in my family and *expect* my children to cooperate. In the heat of battle—in the midst of one of those interminable whiny days—I can become so beleaguered that I unintentionally allow the kids set the tone instead of me.

I don't win every day, and every day is not a happy one

in the Thompson house, but I figure that as long as I keep fighting, and as long as I win more than I lose, I'm on the right path toward making our home the Happy House!

BUILDING BLOCKS

☐ Toddler-friendly devotional idea: To teach our children to warmly greet people when they come into our home, we read Proverbs 15:30a: "A cheerful look brings joy to the heart." We took a few minutes demonstrating "cheerful looks." Then we practiced welcoming people when they come to the door; the kids found it thrilling to take turns knocking on the front door and greeting one another with smiles and hugs. (And yes, we had to practice what this chapter preaches: At one point in our devotional, both older kids ended up in time-out, leaving Kevin and me feeling—and looking!—ridiculous as we danced and sang "Father Abraham" to an oblivious six-month-old.) In spite of the devotional's low point, we ended up having a great time, and the kids got the point. When a friend arrived the next morning, my son stomped off, shouting "No," but when I reminded him about giving cheerful looks, he returned and flashed his gorgeous smile! One small step toward becoming the Happy (and Hospitable) House.

☐ Philippians 2:14–16
Do everything without complaining or arguing, so that you may become blameless and pure, children of God without fault in a crooked and depraved generation, in which you shine like stars in the universe as you hold out the word of life.

I Like You Best

Elizabeth Laing Thompson

After dark, I like you best:

Day fades to gray,
Moonlit fingers paint stripes across your bed, your face.
I tiptoe in and rest a palm across your back
to feel you breathe—
up and down, the rise and fall;
I lean in close to breathe the sweet clean milk of you,
to feel the warmth of life
flowing in and out, in and out as you dream.
You sigh.
And I smile—serene, content—
    This is my sunset.

When you're asleep, I like you best.

At day's first light, I like you best:

Dawn brings a gentle scratching,
the swish-swish of chubby elbows and knees and button nose
scrabbling against the sheets.
Then one little grunt, and soon another;
soft coos and squeals crescendo to a chorus
of joyful babbles to salute the day—
my alarm clock.
I shuffle in,
eyes bleary, all-over weary, heart warming—
and peek around the doorframe.
Two bright chipmunk eyes, two black buttons
peer up at me between the slats.
Eyes twinkle, cheeks crinkle, nose wrinkles;
rosebud lips send fireworks sparkling across the morning—
    This is my sunrise.

When you're awake, I like you best.

From my good-morning sunrise to my lullaby sunset
and my every hour in between;
from your first cry to my last breath,
until the echo of us fades, our souls' footprints blow away—

that's when I like you best.

Smiles and Hugs

- Geri -

Jesus reached out his hand and touched the man.

Matthew 8:3

The Power of Touch

One of the most poignant stories in the Bible is the account of Jesus healing a man who had leprosy. When the man approached Jesus and begged to be healed, Jesus responded in a way that is amazing to me. Not only did he heal the man, but he reached out with his hand and touched the man. Leprosy was and still is a horrible, contagious and disfiguring disease, and at that time, it was incurable. Yet, Jesus touched him!

Jesus had the spiritual power to heal disease and forgive sin, and he could exercise that power from up-close, from far-off and any way he chose. But most of the time he chose to minister to others with physical human touch. When he healed Peter's mother-in-law, "he touched her hand and the fever left her" (Matthew 8:15). "People brought all their sick to him and begged him to let the sick just touch the edge of his cloak, and all who touched him were healed" (Matthew14:35–36). What does this say to us? There is great power in human touch!

I am reminded of the time when Sam was about to have the first of several knee surgeries. Up until that time, he had never been in a hospital, had never been put under anesthesia, and had never had surgery of any kind. Lying in the room before surgery, he began to get more and more anxious until the doctor walked in. The doctor talked to him about the procedure, put his hand on Sam's knee and told him that everything would be fine. Sam still remembers the calming effect of that touch and those words. It was as if the doctor's confidence and concern were passed on to Sam through the reassuring touch to his knee. He would be fine and he was.

So much is communicated by touch—warmth, love, confidence, sympathy, empathy. Touch has an amazing power that transcends words. How easy it is to forget that! For most of us our lives are busy. Even with our children, we can become so consumed with all of the things we must do that we forget to hug them, to give a gentle pat or caress, or to hold them quietly for a few moments.

Touch doesn't take a lot of time, but it pulls us back to one another. Even as my children got older, they needed my hugs and touch. I had to be careful not to embarrass them, and I had to remember to treat them with the respect due them as older children, but it always surprised me how much power an embrace or a gentle pat still had. Sometimes they would "melt" into the hug; at other times they stopped only for a moment, but seemed to leave with a little more confidence and joy.

Today, give your children an extra hug or two. Impart a little more of your love for them with touch.

> And he took the children in his arms, put his hands on them and blessed them. (Mark 10:16)

The Power of a Smile

> A happy heart makes the face cheerful. (Proverbs 15:13)

Our new granddaughter, Avery, has just started smiling.

What a wonderful thing it is to watch her entire face light up as she smiles. Starting at the corners of her mouth and spreading to her eyes, her smiles are heartwarming and contagious. When she smiles, we all smile, and we will do anything to encourage her to smile again! I've often wondered if her smiles are as much the result of inward laughter at our crazy antics as they are from sheer joy.

Don't underestimate the power of a smile. The Bible says that "a cheerful look brings joy to the heart" (Proverbs 15:30). A smile can lift up a discouraged heart and can make someone feel loved, valued or understood. A smile connects people to one another. A warm smile can warm up an entire room of people; it can change the atmosphere of an office, a classroom or a family.

We don't think a lot about smiling. Usually smiles are almost involuntary reactions to something that is funny or that makes us happy. Some of us smile more readily while others have a more serious countenance. We're not angry; we're not sad; we're just not smiling! We can get so busy with life, concentrating on the task at hand or hurrying through our days that we can look so serious—even intimidating.

I want to encourage you to smile. I've noticed that when I purposely smile more, several things happen. First, as I smile, my own heart becomes more joyful. Some of the times when I do not feel very happy at all, I *make* myself smile at other people, and I am always amazed at how quickly my own mood is lifted! Second, I am always surprised at how a smile affects other people. When I smile, people respond! They smile! What I give to others ends up coming back to me. I feel connected to people, and I experience the satisfaction of seeing them "light up," and become happier themselves.

Jonathan reminded me of the power of a smile when he was a little boy. He told me that when he was at school and felt lonely or sad, he would think of me smiling at him, and he would feel better. When I heard that, it made me want to be sure that I smiled even more at my children!

A smile costs nothing, but is a priceless gift of love and joy. Smile at your children. Smile often. Smile with a warmth that reaches out and touches their souls. Those smiles will be carried by them in their hearts long after they are given.

BUILDING BLOCKS

☐ Be very conscious of smiling more today. Smile at your children, at your husband, at complete strangers as you go about your day. How do they respond? How do you feel at the end of the day? (Now—do it again tomorrow!)

☐ Psalm 44:3, emphasis added
It was not by their sword that they won the land,
    nor did their arm bring them victory;
it was your right hand, your arm,
    and *the light of your face*, for you loved them.

Playing Referee
- Elizabeth -

How good and pleasant it is
   when brothers live together in unity!

Psalm 133:1

I might as well suit up in a black-and-white jersey, because some days I feel like a full-time referee. Blake shoves Cassidy out of his way, and I cry, "Personal foul!" Cassidy snatches Blake's toy, and I shout, "Time out!"

The Bible acknowledges the conflicts inherent in sibling relationships. The world's first pair of brothers didn't fare so well—Cain killed Abel out of jealousy in Genesis 3. Then in Genesis 37, Joseph's older brothers sold him into slavery...and siblings have been struggling ever since. So when you and I face difficulties in raising our kids to love (and like!) each other, God understands what we're up against. And yet he gives us hopeful examples as well: Two pairs of brothers—Peter and Andrew, and James and John—served among the twelve apostles. A group of siblings from Bethany—Martha, Mary and Lazarus—were Jesus' devoted friends. And yet, even with their closeness to Jesus, the sisters still had familial conflict to work out, with Jesus' help! (See Luke 10:38–42 and John 11.)

The Scriptures give me hope in the midst of my kids' skirmishes. I also draw confidence from my own experience growing up: To this day, my brothers and sister are my favorite people in the world. When the entire Laing family is all together in one room, all is right with my world. Close families, with brothers and sisters who genuinely love one another, are possible!

My husband and I realize that having three children so close in age presents unique challenges. I keep telling myself that one day I'll be *really* glad I had my kids so close together—of course, I'm glad now (most of the time!), but one day I imagine that it will be a blast to have three potty-trained kids who share similar abilities and interests. (I just pray the girls' interest is not in the same boy...)

Kevin and I are not alone in raising kids who are close in age: Many of today's parents are having their children a bit closer together than in generations past. For most of my mommy friends, two years is the average space between their kids. And fertility treatments have given our generation an astounding number of multiples. Raising two or more toddlers/preschoolers is not for the faint of heart—and heaven help us all when we have multiple teenagers in the house!

But our family life doesn't have to be miserable as our kids mature! Kevin and I get excited when we anticipate family camping trips during the elementary school years, and parties at our house when the Thompson Trio hits the church middle school ministry—but we know that if we don't lay the groundwork for closeness now, our home will never become the teen party zone we envision. These early years are crucial: The atmosphere and patterns we establish, the standards and convictions we instill, the feelings and dynamics we allow—all these will comprise the foundation of our future family life. The preteen and teen years won't be a breeze, but if we put the work in now, the hormonal years won't be nearly as difficult as they *could* be.

If this sounds overwhelming, take heart: Although sibling dynamics can have many layers and complexities, the solution is simpler than we think. My friend Essy, a mother of two, recently put it this way: "We focus on teaching our kids to care about each other's hearts." My parents used to put it a bit more bluntly: "We're going to love each other if it kills us!" The emphasis is the same: We want our children to understand, as their awareness of other people increases, that their siblings have feelings.

We won't be able to monitor or correct every little interaction our kids have, but if we can teach them the overarching lesson of caring about each other, then the appropriate behavior will naturally follow. They will learn to speak kindly, because they don't want to hurt one another; they will learn to share, because they want each other to be happy. If we simply focus on fostering genuine compassion in our children's hearts, then we will lay a strong foundation on which to build our family life.

Of course, this is profound stuff for a self-consumed two-year-old. Toddlers have little concept of compassion or empathy, little sense that anyone's feelings or needs are important besides their own. To them, everyone else is just an accessory in their self-centric world; a supporting actor to their own starring role. One of parents' most important jobs during these early years is to teach our kids that they are not the center of the universe, that other people matter and have feelings and needs.

Kevin and I are just beginning to see signs of hope with our kids—indications that our efforts are planting the right seeds. I love seeing the kids' growing affection for each other, the quirky little relationships they are building. Nothing warms my heart more than to hear my children giggling together. (Of course, the moment I hear their delighted squeals, I brace myself, because within two minutes—without fail—someone gets injured. I'm not kidding.) "Tassie" (Cassidy) is Blake's best bud, and his face lights up when he sees her. He has suddenly decided that it's fun to take turns, and he likes to jump out of her way, saying, "Tassie turn!" When the kids are separated for a while, Cassidy will come to me and say, "But Mommy, I need Blakey. I'm lonely!" And as threatened as she sometimes feels by her brother the toy thief, Cassidy has a compassionate disposition. As soon as Blake gets injured—every two to three minutes, these days—she rushes to comfort him, saying, "I'll take care of you."

Even Avery is getting old enough to "enjoy" the bonding: Just last week, Blake grabbed her pacifier and sucked on it, then shoved it back into her mouth, turned to me and proudly declared, "I sharing!" (And yes, she woke up with a cold the next morning. Great germ sharing, Blake.)

I am still trying to find the balance between intervening and letting my kids work out some conflicts on their own. At this point, they aren't quite mature enough to resolve their own disagreements. I know that I cannot remain their referee forever—one day, I will need to become more of a facilitator of conflict resolution—but for now, I have to stay involved. My primary concern is to prevent bullying behavior and to thwart unhealthy patterns of competitiveness, resentment and animosity.

I am realizing that, because my kids are so close in age, they get along much better when they get short breaks from each other. Human children were not meant to be raised in litters! Sometimes Cassie needs to build block towers all by herself, free from the constant fear that her little brother is about to knock them down; sometimes Blake needs

Mommy's lap all to himself. If I can send one child off with Kevin to run errands, or arrange for one to spend some special time with a friend or a relative—even just for an hour— they get along much better when they are reunited! If your kids are especially close in age, can you give them some time apart (and time alone with you), once every other week or so? The break will do you all some good!

Moms, although we can't dictate or fix every interaction our kids have, let's not ignore the problems when they occur. Let's stay on top of them. And when we do catch our children sharing or doing kind things, let's make a big deal out of it! Clap, dance, hug, give them rewards—whatever it takes to make them excited and proud of their loving behavior.

My prayer for my kids and yours is that all of them will be close, both as a group and one-on-one; both now and always.

BUILDING BLOCKS

☐ Toddler-friendly devotional idea: We recently recounted the story of baby Moses and his big sister, Miriam, and how Miriam watched out for her little brother when he was floating in the Nile River. Then we let the kids take turns being covered in a basket, floating down the Nile. (In our version there were crocodiles, snakes and rapids... Poor baby Moses had a rough go of it!) We used the story to encourage them to watch out for each other and take care of each other. Avery made happy pterodactyl noises from her swing; Blake cared only about rolling around in the basket; but Cassidy actually seemed to grasp the point.

☐ 1 John 2:10, 3:12, 16

Whoever loves his brother lives in the light, and there is nothing in him to make him stumble.... Do not be like Cain, who belonged to the evil one and murdered his brother. And why did he murder him? Because his own actions were evil and his brother's were righteous.... This is how we know what love is: Jesus Christ laid down his life for us. And we also ought to lay down our lives for our brothers.

Superwoman Syndrome

- Geri -

Even youths grow tired and weary, and young men
    stumble and fall;
    but those who hope in the LORD will renew their
    strength.
They will soar on wings like eagles;
    they will run and not grow weary,
    they will walk and not be faint.

Isaiah 40:30–31

I've got news for some of you: Superwoman is not real! She is a fictional hero who inspired and entertained us, but existed only in comic books, on TV and in the movies. The beautiful woman we watched was in make-up and costume, but when she went home she was a woman just like you and me.

Since the late 60s and 70s women have been striving to be seen as strong, capable and equal to men. We have been urged to dream big; we have been told that we can do anything we put our minds to, and that we can have it all. As one who became a young adult in the midst of these decades, I, too, believe that we can do great things with our lives, that life is exciting and rich and waiting for us to leave our mark, but the downside to this is that we have put unrealistic pressures on ourselves. We are trying to be Superwomen! This has especially carried into our lives as mothers, resulting in mothers of young children who are stressed, guilty and exhausted. Instead of enjoying life, they are exhausted and overwhelmed, and they feel inadequate.

I have a little saying that I repeated over and over again to my children and to myself whenever any of us were weighed down in our lives. I have heard them repeat it to others now that they are grown. It is not poetic or even very profound, but it is true: You can only do what you can do! All I can do in this life is the best that I can do, and that will have to be enough.

And honestly, what "I can do" is different for each one of us. I marvel at some of the women I know—how many things they are able to do and do well. And they make it look so easy! They work full time, laboring at jobs of great responsibility, and they keep their homes clean and organized, and have happy husbands and children. Amazing! But not all of us are like that. And that is okay. Each of us can only do our best to live our life and that is enough! We can grow, learn to do new things and do some things better, but we cannot spend all of our lives being stressed out, guilty and unhappy because we cannot do everything as perfectly or as well as someone else.

And...we have to remember: There really is no Superwoman. She is fiction. Even those women who appear so together have their own areas of weakness and insecurity. Everybody does!

The principle that I have learned to live by is this: "I can only take on as much as I can personally handle and still act like a Christian." It is amazing how this little principle helps to clarify my life. It determines the kind of job I accept, how much I time I devote to my work, the kinds of friends I hang out with, and everything else that I do. Especially in my role as wife and mother, I need to "act like a Christian." And if I am allowing myself to live under a degree of pressure that I cannot manage graciously and still treat my family as God wants, then something must change. Either I must grow in my ability to handle the situation, or I must change the situation itself.

It may be that you have held yourself to a standard that is impossible to attain, and so you feel guilty all of the time. All you can see are your failures and inadequacies with your family, your job, your friendships and in your Christian commitment. I will say again: You can only do what you can do. You will not be perfect, you will make mistakes, but do your best. And when you do fail, admit it, get up and keep trying.

You will make mistakes, and I have to tell you, try though you might, you will keep on making them. Don't be overcome with guilt every time you don't measure up perfectly! Like every parent, I made a lot of mistakes with my children, but I loved them and I made sure they knew it. I drew great peace from the promise that "love covers over a multitude of sins" (1 Peter 4:8).

It may be that you are trying to do too much and you need to slow down and take stock. Life can be a harsh and demanding taskmaster, but we don't have to be its slaves! We live in a world that seems to move faster and faster with each passing year. I see many young families running from one thing to the next, so busy and frantic that they are not even able to enjoy each other.

I urge you to take a step back and think. How are you handling life's demands and pressures? Sometimes we need to stop and consider what we are doing and how we are living, and whether all of the things we are committed to are really that important. A good way to measure is to ask ourselves, "Is my family's involvement in this activity really going to matter ten, twenty or thirty years from now?"

There is no Superwoman and we are not Supermoms. Decide what you can do and still be the woman that God wants you to be, and that your husband and children need you to be. Stop measuring yourself by the standards of the world or the accomplishments of others. Run your race. Do the best that you can. When you fall down, get back up, brush yourself off and keep going. You may not run the fastest, and your form may not be perfect, but keep going and you will finish strong: close to God, surrounded by people who love you. What else matters?

> Her children arise and call her blessed;
> her husband also, and he praises her. (Proverbs 31:28)

BUILDING BLOCKS

☐ Where does your Mommy Guilt come from? Is it because you are putting too much pressure on yourself, or is there something specific that you need to repent of, change or get help with?

☐ 2 Thessalonians 3:16
Now may the Lord of peace himself give you peace at all times and in every way. The Lord be with all of you.

Dream Job

- Elizabeth -

He settles the barren woman in her home
as a happy mother of children.

Psalm 113:9

I used to be a productive person. I mean, really, I was amazing—and I bet you were too! And now there are days when I barely make it out of my pajamas. I'm still up early and cranking all day, but if you ask me what I did yesterday, I couldn't really say—except that I never sat down once, and come bedtime, I fell asleep before my husband turned out the light!

One of the major temptations of motherhood is to feel that our new life is not as meaningful or productive as our old life; to wonder whether we are still useful to God, when we can hardly get out of the house.

But God deeply values and even honors our daily work as mothers. Proverbs 31:10–31, the famous passage praising hardworking wives and mothers, is such a testament to the value of what we do. Verse 27 says, "She watches over the affairs of her household and does not eat the bread of idleness." I don't know about you, but I hardly have time to eat, and if I do eat, I am sure the bread of idleness would have far too many carbs to help me lose my baby weight!

But seriously, the passage describes a God-fearing wife and mother as she goes about her daily duties of cooking and cleaning and clothing her family, and it concludes by saying, "Many women do noble things, but you surpass them all." What an encouragement! This is how God feels about our work as wives and mothers. It is invaluable—noble, even. I don't always feel noble when I'm playing referee to two- and three-year-olds while changing a four-month-old's stinky diaper, but God says that I am.

Don't you love the way strangers treat you when you are pregnant? (Okay, except for the uninvited belly rubbing!) They smile at you, open doors for you, give up their seats for you. It's really touching. (And also rather disconcerting when the baby is born and all that attention immediately vanishes and goes to the baby!) God has put something inside every person that values and honors motherhood and the newness of life.

When I was pregnant, if someone ever caught me sitting down resting, I'd laugh and say, "Don't mind me; I'm just sitting here growing a human being." Or sometimes Kevin would ask what I did that day, and I'd smile and say, "Oh, not much, I just grew a new person—you know…" Bringing life into the world and caring for children are precious privileges and weighty tasks.

When people ask us if we work full time, we should all answer, "Yes; in fact I work overtime, and I have my dream job!" Motherhood is a nonstop, full-time job, and I am proud of my occupation. Sure, like many of you, I also have another job a few hours a week, writing and running my editing business, but we moms know where our most important work is done: at home, all alone, where no one sees or applauds (or pays us!).

We cannot fall prey to the temptation to compare our current "productivity" with that of our pre-kid lives—those days will come again as our kids grow older and we resume more rhythm to our lives. Let no one (including your own internal critic!) belittle the work you do in caring for your family and running your home. Titus 2:4–5 says that being busy at home is a godly thing for women to do; and not only does it please God, it is also a testimony to others. On days when we are "stuck" at home, busy raising the kids whom God has entrusted to us, we are doing exactly what God would have us do at this juncture in our lives! When we miraculously find the time to mop a floor, we are doing so to the glory of God, and he is smiling down on us.

No, we probably cannot do all the things we used to do—certainly not for ourselves, and not even for others and for the church—but for now, our *children* are our primary ministry. They are the most important "non-Christians" we will ever spend time with.

Sure, I am trying to share my faith and reach out to people who don't know Christ, but my own children are just now developing a faith in God and a knowledge of his Son—and their conversions will be the most important and heart-rending in which I ever participate. Every day I am molding their characters, shaping their convictions, preparing them for life outside our little haven.

You and I are on the front lines of battle as we raise the next generation, not just of the human race, but of the kingdom of God. We are producing the most precious "commodity" on earth: godly, respectful, potty-trained human beings! If that's not a job that changes the world, I don't know what is.

BUILDING BLOCKS

☐ Before you go to bed tonight, list off in your mind all the things you accomplished today. You may be pleasantly surprised. Even if you only managed to keep everyone's bodies clothed, bottoms clean and bellies content—for most of the day, anyway!—you have achieved a herculean feat. But I'd bet you also did some dishes, straightened a room or two, washed some clothes, made a phone call, sent some e-mails, built your preschooler's confidence, and gave your husband a listening ear. Not a bad day at all! Pat yourself on the back for being such a productive person.

☐ Titus 2:4–5
Then they can train the younger women to love their husbands and children, to be self-controlled and pure, to be busy at home, to be kind, and to be subject to their husbands, so that no one will malign the word of God.

Little Einsteins

- Elizabeth -

My heart is not proud, O LORD,
    my eyes are not haughty;
I do not concern myself with great matters
    or with things too wonderful for me.
But I have stilled and quieted my soul;
    Like a weaned child with its mother,
    like a weaned child is my soul within me.
O Israel, put your hope in the LORD,
    both now and forevermore.

Psalm 131

The pressure on today's mothers to produce little well-rounded geniuses is enormous. And yet it is becoming such an intrinsic part of our cultural attitude that we don't *realize* how much burden we feel, and that it is a fairly new phenomenon.

I love the scene in the 1980s movie *Baby Boom* where all of the yuppie mothers are sitting around the playground consoling a friend whose child did not get into a prestigious preschool. Devastated, the mother is sure that her infant's chances of getting into the Ivy League and having a successful career are now shot. The scene is meant to be funny—and perhaps it was in the 80s—but now it's only a mild exaggeration of a more pervasive mindset.

Think about just a few of the ideals urged upon us:

Breastfeed for at least a year. (And if you do bottle-feed, avoid plastic bottles—they might cause cancer!) Feed your toddlers a perfect rainbow of organic fruits and vegetables. (Corn syrup in the label? Run away screaming!) Don't neglect iron, fluoride and DHA supplements. (But beware too much DHA—it can lead to mercury contamination!) If we do any less, we risk sabotaging our kids' academic success, or frying their developing neurons altogether.

Moms are encouraged to expose babies to classical music in the womb; to read to them daily, beginning in the hospital; to begin teaching word recognition at three months (Don't believe me? Google it!); to introduce art, foreign languages and computers by the age of two—and heaven forbid we ever turn on *Sesame Street* so we can take a shower or cook a meal!

Toys are no longer just toys; they all must serve some educational purpose. Pick up a magazine for baby or toddler parents, and within moments, you may begin to feel like a failure.

Certainly, I am indulging in a bit of hyperbole here, for humor's sake—but I would guess that many young moms have felt some of the pressure I'm talking about. Maybe you have a higher guilt threshold than I do—but I have to consciously keep my Mommy Guilt under control. My goal in writing this chapter is not to discourage you from reading with your kids or feeding them healthy food, but to alleviate some of the anxiety and burden that we guilty souls can feel.

There is no way we can keep up with all the parenting guidelines and early education ideals that society encourages (and that we mothers often endorse). Being a mother was already a full-time job *before* we added in so many new requirements—now it feels impossible! And most young moms work outside the home at least part time. If we constantly pressure ourselves to be a flawless breadwinner/gourmet health-food chef/educator extraordinaire, we won't have time to nurture our own marriages, friendships and sanity. By expecting so much of ourselves and each other, we give ourselves no choice: Our world *must* revolve entirely around our children!

Even if we don't pressure ourselves to constantly educate our little ones, we may feel obligated to always *entertain* our kids. We push ourselves to continuously stimulate our infants and engage with our toddlers, afraid to squander a moment. We feel guilty if we do something for ourselves—even necessary tasks such as housework or returning a phone call—when our children want to play with us...which is every minute that they are awake!

My mom helps me to relax by giving me gentle reminders that all-day, in-your-face stimulation is overwhelming for babies—even infants need quiet time to themselves! And when I read *John Rosemond's New Parent Power,* I realized that constantly playing with my toddlers would do them a disservice. One of our jobs as mothers is to teach our kids to be independent and to entertain themselves at times.

I recently had a conversation with someone who described, in passing, some of the cool classes and programs that her kids are enrolled in, and I couldn't figure out why I felt stressed out and guilty for days afterwards. I finally realized that I was pressuring myself to keep up, and that I was worrying about depriving my children of developmental and social opportunities. But the fact is, Kevin and I cannot afford many extra classes and programs, and my mobility is limited right now, with all my kids so young. There is nothing wrong with any of the things this other mother is doing for her kids—they are great activities, and their family enjoys them—but I realized that I do not have to keep up, and neither do my kids. What works for other families may not work for us.

If comparing notes with other moms begins to feel competitive or stressful rather than helpful, just change the subject. If perusing a parenting magazine makes you feel inadequate, just put down the magazine. During my last pregnancy, every time I picked up a pregnancy magazine I began to worry about bizarre birth defects and feel overly paranoid about what I ate. (You'd think I would have gotten past the paranoia by the third pregnancy, right?) I finally put down the magazines and drove straight to Starbucks for the best therapy I know: a decaf, nonfat, no-whip mocha! I used common sense in what I ate, and you know what? Avery Grace turned out fine, and I did not gain a bajillion pounds!

Having said all that, don't get me wrong. I am a big fan of reading with kids, of teaching them age-appropriate lessons, and feeding them organic food—but I have decided to take the pressure off myself and to stop feeling guilty all the time. If I can inspire my children to be curious and to love learning, they will do great in school and in life. Kevin and I read with our kids because we all enjoy it, not because we feel compelled to teach them how to read before kindergarten. We have fun teaching colors, shapes, letters and numbers—but we do it casually, and not because we are "bad parents" if we don't.

My faith and awe of God grows as I explain the wondrous workings of creation to my wide-eyed children—how the seasons change and the bees pollinate the flowers; how the rain makes the plants bloom and God makes babies grow inside their mommies (but not how he puts them there...we'll save that lesson for a few more years!). I love educational games like blocks and puzzles—but I also love the swing set and dress-up and running around and playing in the dirt. (Okay, I don't love the laundry afterwards, but in theory, I like the dirt thing.)

A perfect mother does not exist. Chances are, our children will turn out fine, both because *and* in spite of us! A little television, in modest amounts, will not destroy their neurons. A cookie here and there is good for the soul, if not the body. If our kids can't quote *The Iliad,* sight-read Mozart, and take apart a motherboard before they hit first grade, they can still thrive in school. We have no one to impress; there is no standard our kids must live up to, and our confidence and happiness do not depend upon their accomplishments.

And hey—if we really do want our kids to be little Einsteins, let's keep in mind that when Einstein himself was a student—well, some say he was no Einstein! Maybe there's hope for our little underachievers, after all.

BUILDING BLOCKS

☐ Need a few minutes to yourself today? Try my friend Sarah's timer trick: Set the kitchen timer for five or ten minutes, and tell your kids to play without you until the timer goes off. Gradually increase their independent play time to fifteen or twenty minutes.

☐ 1 Corinthians 1:20
Where is the wise man? Where is the scholar? Where is the philosopher of this age? Has not God made foolish the wisdom of the world?

A Kiss and a Promise

Elizabeth Laing Thompson

Tonight I kissed a promise
As we said good night;
I nuzzled cheeks with gentle lips,
And squeezed fat fingers tight.

I kissed heaven's promise,
A future yet unfurled,
A kicking, cooing bundle
Of hopes, such precious pearls—
All that can and might and should
Come true within this world.

Tonight I kissed a promise,
Gave one last bedtime pat,
And when I kissed that chubby cheek,
God kissed me right back.

Let Them Play

- Geri -

There is a time for everything,
and a season for every activity under heaven....
A time to weep and a time to laugh,
a time to mourn and a time to dance.

Ecclesiastes 3:1, 4

Sam and I once tried to count the number of "Big Wheels" that we had put together in our lives as parents. We lost count after eleven. I will never forget the myriad of parts spread out over the floor as we tried to follow directions that were not only complicated and confusing, but usually written in or translated from another language. Many Christmas Eves were spent assembling toys, and finally getting to bed just a couple of hours before the children woke up on Christmas morning. Even as I think back today, the memories are exhausting, but precious.

I especially remember how much David loved riding his Big Wheel. He literally burned the soles off the bottom of his sneakers by using his feet as brakes. The greatest punishment we could give David was not allowing him to ride his Big Wheel. He endowed his Big Wheel with lifelike qualities. I still smile as I remember him saying to his little friend Luke, "Let's park our Big Wheels next to each other so they can talk!"

Children love to play and they *need* to play. Play allows

them to exercise their bodies, use their minds and develop their imaginations. The most mundane things that only signify work to us can be turned into objects of play. Pots and pans become wonderful musical instruments; in the world of a child, a kitchen can be turned into a symphony hall.

It concerns me the extent to which we have taken away free and imaginative play from our children. Nowadays, much of the time of our young ones is structured, and their play is controlled by adults. While there is a place for organization and structure, my experience and my instincts tell me we have gone too far.

For years I taught preschool children from ages eighteen months to four years old. We provided several activities each day in which they sat in a group and had stories and sang songs, which taught them how to sit still and pay attention for short periods of time. As they got older, they began to draw and to learn their colors, letters and numbers. But in the midst of these organized activities we also made a conscious effort to let them have unstructured times as well. They played indoors and outdoors, and, although they were carefully supervised, they were allowed to run free and just be children.

It is my observation that many young mothers feel guilty if they are not personally playing with or interacting with their children just about every waking hour. While lots of love and contact with Mom is needed, realize that you do not need to be your children's personal playmate! You are their mother! The role you have in their lives is one of loving, protecting, nurturing and training—not necessarily entertaining. In fact, those of you who work or have more than one child will not have the luxury of having large chunks of time to just "play." That does not mean you are a bad mother. You need to watch, listen and be ready to help or intervene when necessary, but *let them play*!

The time that children have in unstructured play is invaluable. As they interact with their own little world, their imaginations develop and they learn lessons that can't be taught in a classroom. As they play with others they learn how to get along, to share, to resolve conflict and to express themselves. When they play alone, they learn the invaluable skill of entertaining themselves, and what it means to be comfortable with who they are.

Let your children play sometimes—no, *lots* of times—without being coached or wearing a uniform. Every sport doesn't have to be organized; every game doesn't have to have a winner! Let them make up their own games; let them run and jump and shout! While there certainly is a place for organized activities and sports, let's not make it too much of the time, especially when our kids are very young.

Let your kids play outside. What a beautiful world we live in; what an incredible playground God has made for our children! I remember my kids spending so many delightful hours outside riding their Big Wheels and bikes—first on the driveway and then graduating to the cul-de-sac. I can still see them playing for hours on the swing set in the back yard and floating their plastic boats in the stream right next to our house. It was really just a little brook with only a few inches of water in it, but to them it was a mighty river.

At first I was right there with them, but as they got older, I watched from the window. And as I listened, I often laughed at the funny conversations they had with one another. Their conversations would at times get ugly or heated, and I had an opportunity to correct and teach, and sometimes I had to call them back inside. But those years of learning about the world by playing in it were precious and invaluable for my kids. I still smile as I recall those memories, and I deeply believe much of who my children are today was learned from their times of outdoor play.

There are some wonderful programs on television that teach and entertain even the youngest children, and I am all for them in limited amounts, but television and computers cannot be a child's only—or primary—means of play. Kids need the physical and creative exercise of "real" play as well as the personal interactions that go along with it.

Not only do your children benefit from free play, but you do, too! A child who runs and plays is a child who at the end of the day is tired and ready for sleep. And while they are busy playing, you have some precious moments of quiet and peace, or you can get some things done! You can fix dinner, fold clothes, make a phone call. And, when your children are active and busy, they will not be as likely to whine that they are bored and beg every five minutes for food. My experience has been that the harder my children played, the better their appetites were at mealtime, and the less mindless snacking they did.

I realize that many mothers of young children work and come home at the end of the day with just enough time to feed and bathe exhausted children before bedtime. Hopefully the kids have had times to have fun during the day, and you can play with them in the evening and have some special playtime during the weekends. But even on those off days when you are at home, although they need you and your devoted attention, they still need time to be on their own. And you still need time to carry out the endless duties of running a household.

The Bible says, "When I was a child, I spoke like a child,

I reasoned like a child. When I became a man, I put childish ways behind me" (1 Corinthians 13:11). Children will grow up soon enough. Although it may not seem like it right now, they are young for only a few precious years. These are the years for them to live free and without care. Maybe we need to get out of their way a bit more. They need to run, skip and be silly; they need to sing, to make up games and live life with exuberance and abandon. Let's let them and let's enjoy it along with them! While our children are young, let's allow them plenty of time to be children, to have fun and to just...play!

BUILDING BLOCKS

☐ Play a game of "Let's Pretend." Pretend that there are no televisions, no DVD players, no video games. What would you do to have fun? Let the kids come up with some ideas; then do them! A couple of ideas: Blow up one balloon and see how many games you can invent with it (before it pops!). Or how about a ball or even a piece of wadded up paper and a bowl or a bucket? What can you come up with?

☐ John 10:10
"I have come so that they may have life, and have it to the full."

Discipline Starts Early

- Geri -

The LORD disciplines those he loves,
as a father the son he delights in.
                            Proverbs 3:12

Have you ever seen a child throw a temper tantrum in a public place? Or perhaps I should ask, have you ever experienced the embarrassment of your own child throwing a fit while others looked on?

I remember going to the grocery store with all three of my little ones when Jonathan was a toddler. Aside from the fact that it was like a three-ring circus trying to shop with all of them in tow, Jonathan seemed to know that the checkout line was the perfect place for him to assert himself. I was usually hemmed in with people in front and behind, groceries on the counter and nowhere to go when he would begin to demand things. He'd cry, whine and complain, becoming louder and more insistent by the moment. I felt at first embarrassed, then helpless, then out of control, and ended up becoming just plain angry!

Children misbehave. They disobey, whine, cry, fight with each other, and take you on—that is life as a parent. Your kids can make your life miserable...*if you let them!* Our job as parents is to train and teach our offspring to be loving, kind and obedient, and this is something that begins early—earlier than many of us think.

When I taught preschool, I was amazed at just how much young children were able to understand, and how early. Most children are able to comprehend what we say to them long before they themselves are able to verbalize very well. Receptive language always precedes expressive language.

To illustrate just how much young ones can understand, let me tell you a story about the young son of a friend of mine. Joseph was less than eighteen months old and was beginning to resist sitting in his stroller. On one occasion, his mother let him walk around for a few minutes, and when it was time to get back into the stroller, he refused. In warning, she began to count to ten (a practice I do not generally advocate). As his mother recited each successive number, Joseph inched a little closer to his stroller. By the time she got to the number nine, he was standing right beside his stroller, and just before she counted ten, he quickly jumped in and took his seat. I was amazed. Although this child could not yet speak, he understood exactly what was being said and what was expected of him.

What does this mean? Experience teaches us that at a fairly young age we can begin to teach our little ones and expect them to obey. It means that you can say "sit down" or "come here" and anticipate their cooperation. It means that you can expect them to lie still while you are changing their diaper. It means they can understand they are never to kick or hit Mommy or Daddy.

From about eighteen months to five years of age is the time when we must teach our children to obey and respect us. It is here that we establish patterns that lay the foundation for the years to come. To guide us through this time, the Bible has a two-part command that encompasses and supersedes all others: "Children, *obey* your parents in the Lord, for this is right. *Honor* your father and mother..." (Ephesians 6:1-2, emphasis mine). Both expectations—obey and honor—are absolutely necessary, and they balance each other out perfectly. Obedience deals with action, while honor (or respect) addresses the heart behind the action.

Mothers, begin teaching these concepts to your children while they are still young. It is during the Tender Years that our children must be taught to obey and to respect God-given authority beginning with us, their parents, and carrying over to all legitimate authorities in their lives. This task is not always fun, and you will sometimes feel like you are address-ing the same things over and over, but don't give up. The kids will eventually get it, and when they do, it will be well worth the effort.

I can't emphasize it enough: *start early*. The longer we wait, the more difficult it becomes. Habits and behaviors can become established and ingrained, and little hearts can become defiant. Please understand, I am not saying we need to be unreasonable, harsh or abusive. I am saying we must be firm, confident and consistent. To be sure, our little ones need lots of our love and encouragement, but they also need us to teach them what is right, and then to implement our expectations.

God in the Bible speaks often and emphatically to parents about the need to discipline children. The Scriptures teach us that there are many different ways to train them. To be effec-tive, we will need to work towards becoming proficient at various forms of discipline. Raising and shaping our children is not always negative, nor does it always mean punishment; it encompasses training, correcting and holding our children to an expectation and a standard. Sam and I have a compre-hensive discussion of this subject in another book, *Raising*

Awesome Kids—Reloaded.[*]

> For these commands are a lamp;
>> this teaching is a light,
> and the corrections of discipline
>> are the way to life. (Proverbs 6:23)

> Discipline your son, for in that there is hope.
>> Do not be a willing party to his death. (Proverbs 19:18)

Let me share with you young moms a few special tips about disciplining kids during the Tender Years.

- **Choose your battles wisely**. Young children are a work in progress and we cannot discipline them for every little thing. Sometimes battles can be avoided by merely moving or distracting our children. Correct when necessary, but do not make every issue a battle that you must fight and win.

- **Don't always be saying 'no.'** With so much behavior to correct, this is certainly easier said than done. But, try to tune in to your own words, and if you hear yourself constantly saying "no," make some adjustments. Perhaps you can learn to creatively rephrase your wording. Or, when possible, change your child's focus, and just give them something else to do. But, when you do say "no," be sure to mean it and enforce it!

- **Realize that all children, including the 'easy' ones, need discipline**. It is simple to spot the misbehavior of openly defiant children, yet we can be blinded to the disobedience of a seemingly more compliant, complacent

---

[*]*Raising Awesome Kids—Reloaded* (Spring Hill, TN: DPI, 2008), chapter 6.

child. Sometimes, it is our youngest child that we fail to discipline. Perhaps we have just grown weary over time, or it may be that we have forgotten that our older children didn't just automatically grow out of certain behaviors; we helped them along the way.

When David was little, I found it harder to consistently and firmly discipline him. I had learned to be firm and strong with his outspoken older sister, but our son's personality was quite different from hers. He was small for his age, a little shy, and very attached to Mommy. I will never forget one of my friends observing me as I failed to deal with my son, telling me, "Geri, you would never let Elizabeth act like that." And she was right! I came to see that my neglect was going to hurt him. Yes, David needed to be handled differently than his sister, but still he required a firm, loving hand. It is my observation that mothers tend to be weaker in dealing with their sons than with their daughters (and I see the same pattern with fathers and daughters). To overcome this tendency, both Mom and Dad will have to be aware of it, and work diligently to be effective and consistent.

"When is the right time to begin disciplining our children?" is one of the questions most often asked by young parents. Our dear friend, child neuropsychologist Dr. Michael Shapiro, has a great answer for parents who ask this: "as soon as a child is capable of willful disobedience."

❧

As we close our thoughts, I am reminded of a Proverb that gives important insight:

Discipline Starts Early

When I was a boy in my father's house,
  still tender, and an only child of my mother,
he taught me and said,
  "Lay hold of my words with your heart;
  keep my commands and you will live."
(Proverbs 4:3–4, emphasis mine)

The writer takes pains to assure us that his parents taught and trained him in his earliest years, even before his younger siblings came on the scene. Mothers, you can be confident that God expects you to start training your children at a young age. Teach and discipline them with love and patience, and with firmness and consistency. The rewards will be great—for them, and for you as well!

BUILDING BLOCKS

☐ A great little game to teach obedience is "Simon Says." Have fun giving commands and acting them out with each other. You may even change the name of the game to "Mommy Says"!

☐ Proverbs 29:17
Discipline your son, and he will give you peace;
  he will bring great delight to your soul.

Tantrum

Elizabeth Laing Thompson

"No."

Fury flashes—
a mushroom cloud blooms in bright eyes
that sparkled with happy desire
just seconds ago.
Tears rise, balance on eyelids, threatening;
pink lips melt into a frown, distorting,
then open wide to reveal a smattering of pointy white teeth.

A millimoment of silence.
The calm before the storm.
I brace myself.

A wail explodes, full throttle:
shattering eardrums, sanity, and the baby's nap—
A piercing siren screaming your emergency, drowning out the world.
Hot fat tears race down cheeks flushed red with betrayal;
Hands clench into fists, pummeling the air;
Feet stomp a furious rhythm, punishing the carpet.
And still the sound swells—
Ringing, resounding—
Penetrating my bone marrow until, trembling,
I fear I will explode;
And then you are Superman, flying face-first onto the floor...

All because of chocolate milk.

'No' Is Not a Four-Letter Word

- Elizabeth -

"Simply let your 'yes' be 'yes' and your 'no' be 'no.'"
Matthew 5:37

It's no fun saying "no."

The other night, my husband teased me about something silly, and I burst into tears. As he stared at me in bewilderment, I explained that I was on edge because Blake—my good-natured, affectionate boy; my refuge when Cassidy continually vies for my position as Head Woman of the House—had suddenly turned on me. Almost overnight, that all-too-familiar demon, rebellion, had bloomed in my son's beautiful blue eyes. He began staring me down from beneath his to-die-for-mile-long lashes—and deliberately stomping his foot in defiance, just to see how I would react.

By the time bedtime finally arrived, after hours of his little tantrums and Cassidy's clever manipulations, I felt like Public Enemy Number One. My two toddlers had ganged up on me and outnumbered me all day—and I was exhausted. I had won the battles, but lost a bit of my confidence and joy in the process.

Yes, it's no fun saying "no."

One of the college students in our campus ministry recently interned in a local, "progressive" preschool. One day she corrected a little boy who had bitten another boy. She was quickly pulled aside by a supervisor, and told never to say "no" to a child; her boss encouraged her, next time, to simply redirect the boy—to explain that "we bite food, not people." The little biter continued terrorizing his fellow preschoolers for days—but poor Ashley could only tell him, "We bite food, not people!" In frustration, she soon quit her job.

Some child-rearing philosophies would have us believe that "no" is a four-letter word. Common sense says otherwise—and so does God! While I appreciate the wisdom in redirecting and patiently teaching our children, there are times when we have to "just say 'no.'"

Sure, sometimes it's wise to sidestep a run-in with a toddler by distracting them; sure, sometimes it's best to provide our kids a graceful way out of a confrontation, instead of forcing them to say "uncle." As my mom sagely points out in another chapter, "Everything can't be 'no.'" But *some* things *are* "no," and always will be. Period. Biting? No! (I bit my brother once, when I was five. My mom lightly bit me back, and I was so stunned that I never bit anyone again!) Hitting? No! Playing with knives? No! Running into the street? No!

While most moms reading this book may not subscribe to the "never say 'no'" philosophy, I imagine that we all occasionally feel bad for laying down the law for our kids. I hate to see disappointment in my kids' eyes, but they cannot live on chocolate milk and cookies! If all we do is bark "no" all day long, we will have unhappy children—but there is a time for firmness.

When we feel bad for putting our foot down, let us remember some of the hard facts of life: There are some things that we—adults and children alike—simply cannot do.

There is right, and there is wrong. We have laws to obey, authorities to whom we must submit—whether or not we agree with them! Our children will hear the word *no* at times in their life. If we try to shelter them from ever hearing *no* or being disappointed, they will find themselves unprepared for the real world and unhappy in life.

A preacher we know recently spoke at a teen retreat about his parenting style. He said, "Sometimes my kids ask me for things, and I say 'no.' Could I buy it for them? Sure. Do I mind if they have it? Not really. But sometimes, it's just good for them to hear me say 'no!'"

If we don't want to raise spoiled brats—well, we will sometimes have to say "no." Part of our job as mothers is to teach our kids to submit and obey when appropriate; to teach them about life—that, as much as we hate to say it, life is not fair, and that they cannot do everything they want. If they don't hear "no" from us, they are certainly going to hear it elsewhere, so they might as well learn to deal with disappointment and rules within the safety of their family life. Let's prepare our little ones to take some hits, and get back up again!

For those days when you need a confidence booster, don't take my word for it—take God's:

> Do not withhold discipline from a child;
>   if you punish him with the rod, he will not die.
> Punish him with the rod and save his soul from death.
>   My son, if your heart is wise then my soul will be glad.
> (Proverbs 23:13–15)

> Our fathers [and mothers!] disciplined us for a little while, as they thought best; but God disciplines us for our good, that we may share in his holiness. No discipline seems

pleasant at the time, but painful. Later on, however, it produces a harvest of righteousness and peace for those who have been trained by it. (Hebrews 12:10–11, parenthetical addition mine)

God has put us in charge of our children for a reason. We have his permission—and expectation—to teach and train. We don't have to apologize for setting rules and sticking with them. It's not mean to set boundaries, or to refuse to give our children everything they want. *No* doesn't damage their self-esteem; rather, it provides order to their little world—even a sense of comfort and safety.

A friend of mine once discovered her two-year-old son in the kitchen, eating a stick of butter as tears rolled down his cheeks. Holding out the chewed butter blob with his slimy hands, he wailed, "Mommy, come take this away from me!" He knew he was disobeying—perhaps he already felt sick to his stomach!—but he needed his mom to reinforce the house rules and help him escape the temptation.

Although everything can't be *no*, when we do say "no," we must mean it—and that means that we expect obedience. I try not to make rules or commands if I cannot enforce them, because I want my children to know that I mean what I say.

And let me encourage you—when your kids defy you, be strong! My mom is so sweet, she is borderline angelic, but if any of us kids ever disobeyed or sassed her, it was "No More Mrs. Nice Guy!" It's not wrong for Christian women to speak firmly.

Sometimes Cassidy will try to manipulate me when I discipline her. She'll look up at me and say, "Mommy, that's not a nice thing to say." It may not *sound* nice, but it *is* right! Christian mothers can and should speak strongly at times.

It's not wrong to have a no-nonsense, "you're in big trouble Mister" tone of voice and facial expression; otherwise, a strong-willed child will walk right over us!

So let's don our armor, stiffen our spines and draw the parenting battle lines wherever our kids need them. Go ahead, just say "no"! One day, your kids may actually thank you for it.

BUILDING BLOCKS

☐ Want some more great reading about parenting when you're finished reading this book? Try Dr. James Dobson's *Dare to Discipline* and *The Strong-Willed Child*. Also try John Rosemond's *New Parent Power*, Douglas and Vicki Jacoby's *The Quiver* and my parents' book, *Raising Awesome Kids—Reloaded*.

☐ Proverbs 13:24
He who spares the rod hates his son,
but he who loves him is careful to discipline him.

Soundtrack

Elizabeth Laing Thompson

Giggles and coos,
    Babbles and toots;
Hiccups and chirps,
    Yodels and burps;
Feed-me-now squeals,
    Belly-laugh peals;
Nasal drip-drops,
    Coughs, squirts and pops;

Song all the day,
    Music by night;
Dance of our souls,
    Soundtrack of life.

Broken Record

- Elizabeth -

My son, keep your father's commands
    and do not forsake your mother's teaching.
Bind them upon your heart forever;
    fasten them around your neck.
When you walk, they will guide you;
    when you sleep, they will watch over you;
    when you awake, they will speak to you.

Proverbs 6:20-22

"Get off the table! Thank you, good job. Hey—no!—don't jump off the couch! Thank you, that's better, good boy, that's wonderf—Wait! No, please don't rub your face on my good pillows—your boogers—aw, gross! Hey—don't snatch that toy from your sister! No, I said don't snatch! Don't even think about snatching! Oh, no you don't—don't you dare hit. If you hit, you're going to be in big trouble, mister! Did you just stomp your foot at me? We never stomp our feet at Mommy. Oh, now you've done it—when I get off the toilet, you're gonna get it! Hey! Put that down! Not my coffee cup! No! Where are you going? Stop! Freeze! Don't move a muscle! Pleeease give me back my coffee cup? Come back! No, not on my white carpet! AAAAAH!"

Sound familiar? Welcome to thirty seconds of the sound-track at my house. Repeat about fifty times, and some days, you'll have it just about right.

As preschool parents, we can feel doomed to parrot the same instructions over and over and over and over and over again. We issue the same commands, prohibitions and lectures all day long; we punish for the same offenses day after day; we address the same character and behavior concerns for weeks on end. We get creative—we read Bible verses; give rewards; tell stories; sing songs; buy books that teach moral lessons; perform stuffed-animal reenactments—but still the behavior persists. We feel like a broken record.

But we can't give up! Sometimes, repetition is exactly what our kids need. They must know that we are serious, and that they can't change our minds or wear down our resolve over time. Why else do you think Deuteronomy 6 commands us to employ so many different ways of teaching our children about God's laws—by tying them as symbols on our hands and foreheads *and* by talking about them at home *and* when we walk along the road *and* when we lie down *and* when we get up *and* by writing them on our doorframes and gates? Because we need the repetition!

When we feel like broken records with our kids, when we feel ignored and begin to wonder whether our children suffer from hearing loss, we are getting just a small taste of how our heavenly Father must sometimes feel with all of his children. How many times does he repeat himself in the Bible? And how many times do we fail to listen? We can hear God's frustration in verses such as Isaiah 42:20:

> You have seen many things,
>   but have paid no attention.
> Your ears are open,
>   but you hear nothing.

Jesus echoed God's sentiments when he said: "O unbelieving and perverse generation, how long shall I stay with you and put up with you?" (Luke 9:41). Let us keep in mind our own failings, our own stubbornness, when we are tempted to throw up our hands in irritation with our little ones. (And yes, I imagine that many of you, like me, are getting genetic repayment for the defiance that we once dished out to our own poor parents!)

In the heat of battle, remember 1 Corinthians 13:5: "Love...keeps no record of wrongs." Even when we are embroiled in a prolonged battle of wills with a headstrong child, we must keep on loving the little terror. I take comfort and guidance from one of my childhood heroines, the sweet troublemaker Anne of Green Gables, who said: "Each day is fresh, with no mistakes in it!" Just as our kids need consistent discipline, they also need the reassurance of a clean slate every morning—and sometimes every hour.

The apostle Paul viewed repetition and reminders as a way of protecting his flock. He said,

> Finally, my brothers, rejoice in the Lord! It is no trouble for me to write the same things to you again, and it is a safeguard for you.... Rejoice in the Lord always. I will say it again: Rejoice! (Philippians 3:1, 4:4)

Reinforcing lessons is a way of protecting our children, of imprinting convictions in their minds so that one day, when they are not with us, our voice will echo in their memories and remind them what to do.

Sure, we should expect our children to listen and obey—even to obey the first time. If we find ourselves constantly addressing the same issue, with no success, then it can't hurt to reconsider our strategy: Are we following through with the consequences we threaten? Would a different approach be more effective? However, even with the most consistent and creative of parenting, some lessons take time to sink in.

Even when kids finally seem to "get it," they are bound to regress at times. Proverbs 22:15 says,

> Folly is bound up in the heart of a child,
> but the rod of discipline will drive it far from him.

Children will naturally return to their default setting— whether it be one of whining, defiance, selfishness or anger—and they often need to be "reset" and reminded of the house rules. They may seem to master a lesson for a while, and just when we think we can relax and breathe, they up and whallop their younger sibling again, just to see if the rules have changed! (Yes, "up and whallop" is a proper grammatical expression with roots in Neo-Southern American Drawl, in case you were wondering.)

But take heart: Your kids are listening more than they let on. I have been encouraged recently by reports that Cassidy quotes me in my absence. In spite of how much she fights me at home, she actually does hear me, and she even values my opinion and convictions. The other day I even heard Blake garble the words "obey" and "spank-spank"—and I knew that he was making some important connections about consequences.

Let's keep at it, and one day, we'll realize that we've gone a whole morning without saying, "Don't hit" or "Don't whine" or "Share"—and we can rejoice in the small (yet oh so monumental) accomplishment. Before long, we may string a few days or weeks together, and enjoy a time of peace...just enough time to gear up for the next parenting quandary!

≈

No matter what child-rearing challenges we face, or how long they take to overcome, let us draw comfort from Paul's encouragement to the church in Galatia: "Let us not become weary in doing good, for at the proper time we will reap a harvest if we do not give up" (Galatians 6:9).

BUILDING BLOCKS

☐ You can't fight every battle at once. What are the top three house rules you are trying to establish or enforce right now? Which one is *most* important?

☐ Psalm 32:8–9
I will instruct you and teach you in the way you should go;
I will counsel you and watch over you.
Do not be like the horse or the mule,
which have no understanding
but must be controlled by bit and bridle
or they will not come to you.

The Bedtime Blessing

- Geri -

> But I have stilled and quieted my soul;
>> like a weaned child with its mother,
>> like a weaned child is my soul within me.
>
> Psalm 131:2

"Bedtime Blessing" is not exactly the way many of you young mothers would describe those last moments of the day as you put your children to bed. The only "blessing" about bedtime is that when the children finally do go to sleep, you can have some peace and quiet! But that is not the blessing that I am speaking about.

A smooth and calm bedtime for children is not impossible, and does not have to be an ordeal that drags on and on. Believe it or not, bedtime can be an occasion of love and peace, a moment of closeness with your children; a time that provides security far beyond the bedtime hour and is remembered long after children are grown.

Here are a few suggestions that may help you make this a more peaceful time.

A Regular Bedtime

Children need routine, and a regular bedtime is a routine that is especially important. If you watch carefully, you will notice that your children will begin to wind down at almost the same time every night. While they may resist and protest that they are not sleepy, your little ones will begin to rub their eyes and get fussy, or perhaps become more energetic and active. God made everyone to require a prolonged time of rest at night, and young children need more than adults. Many times children who are ill-mannered and out of control are just tired and sleepy. They will remain hard to handle unless their parents assert control and provide the routine and rhythm they need.

Establish a regular time that your children go to bed each night. Don't wait until they fall asleep in front of the television or until your own bedtime. Decide on a reasonable time and stick to it. When my children were young, they were usually in bed between 7:30 and 8:00, which allowed Sam and me to have some time alone or to get with other people later in the evening.

You may find that children who have always been quick to fall asleep suddenly begin to have difficulty at bedtime. They are wide awake and resist being put to bed. When this happens, you may need to take a look at their naptimes. As children grow, their patterns change. Are they taking their naps too late in the day or napping for too long? Both of these things can affect their going to sleep at their normal bedtime. If so, you may need to make some changes, either adjusting their naptime or their bedtime. And don't feel like you are being a bad parent when you make some of those adjustments according to what works best for you and your marriage.

Remember this about routine or schedule: When it comes to raising children, there must be some flexibility. There will be times that you are unable to put your children to bed at the normal time. There will be weekly church activities or other important family or social gatherings that you need to attend. Work diligently to establish and keep a normal bedtime for your kids, but remember: Your routine is your servant, not your master.

A Bedtime Ritual

Bedtime will go much more smoothly when you follow a simple ritual every night. It may consist of a bedtime story and a prayer, or a song and prayer, or a little game such as "My favorite thing today was..." or "I love you more than..." Whatever the routine, this is a time when your child needs to feel loved and safe, and to have a relaxing, wind-down time before going to sleep. This doesn't—and, in fact, shouldn't—take very long. The good news is that a routine like this can be followed if your child is put to bed somewhere else or even by someone else. Since the bedtime ritual is the same each night, its familiarity provides children a special comfort and security.

Each of our children had their own special songs that I sang at bedtime. Elizabeth's songs were "Silent Night" and "Now the Day Is Over." Jonathan and Alexandra liked "Jesus Loves Me" (although each one wanted a different verse), and for some unknown reason David insisted on "Baa, Baa Black Sheep."

Even today, when Elizabeth puts her three-year-old daughter, Cassidy, to bed, she follows a routine, and I follow it too when Cassidy stays at our house. It is especially touching to me that some of the songs that Cassidy likes are the same ones I sang to Elizabeth when I used to put her to bed.

There is another little bonus that comes from having a bedtime ritual: When there is a part of bedtime that is pleasant and desirable, it can be used to your advantage. Sometimes kids try to turn bedtime into a power struggle. When my children did this, I would quite pleasantly but firmly say, "The way you are acting shows me how very tired you are. You are probably too tired tonight to have your song or story, so I will just quickly say good night and let you go to sleep right away."

This was always met with an emphatic "No, Mommy! I want my song and story! I'll lie down and be good!"

But there can be other bedtime power struggles: "I want a drink of water!" "I need to go to the bathroom!" "I want the light on!" "I want another kiss!" "Don't leave me!" These and countless other cries and demands can take all of the blessing and peace out of bedtime and keep you running back and forth to your child's bedroom as if you are their personal servants.

A Firm Hand

Mothers, please understand that few children readily and eagerly go to bed. They just don't want to miss whatever might happen, and they honestly don't want to separate from you. For other children, bedtime is also a time to test limits and see who is really in charge.

Bedtime is what you make it. You must establish a pleasant, but firm routine, and you cannot let kids manipulate and exasperate you. Anticipate needs such as drinks and trips to the bathroom that can be taken care of ahead of time, and then do not give in to their demand for more and more.

Do not argue or cajole. Follow the ritual that you have established, and then lovingly, firmly say good night and leave the room. If they cry, they cry. If they throw a temper tantrum, let them do so by themselves. You can usually figure out if a child is just demanding more from you to exert his or her own control, or if they have a legitimate need. Of course, even when they have a real need, children can quickly learn to use that excuse to get their way at other times. It is up to you take back control at bedtime.

I was reminded of this recently when Elizabeth went through this struggle with Cassidy. Bedtime had been a simple, peaceful ritual that was followed every night. However, as

Cassidy got older, she began to make more and more bedtime demands. At first they seemed reasonable, but eventually bedtime became a lengthy, dreaded and frustrating time of day.

Finally, Elizabeth and Kevin decided to end the misery and help Cassidy to understand exactly "who is in charge." Once they said good night, they refused to go back in to meet her further demands and cries. When she continued to scream and wail for what seemed like forever, they took it even a step further. Cassidy loves all things "princess"; she has princess books, princess movies, princess dolls and her most beloved possessions: princess dresses. Her parents had a talk with her—since Cassidy was not acting anything like a princess in the way she was behaving at bedtime, she could no longer dress like a princess. With great ceremony they carried all of her princess dresses upstairs and hung them in Mommy's closet. Cassidy was told that she would have to earn back the princess dresses, one at a time, by acting like a princess—especially at bedtime.

Well, this got through to Cassidy as nothing else had. She knew that Mommy and Daddy meant business, and she was now motivated to change. It only took a few days of going to bed peacefully before she began to get back her precious princess dresses.

There were two things that Kevin and Elizabeth did that ended the power struggle and the misery: First, they refused to participate on her terms. And second, they came up with a creative way to both discipline and inspire Cassidy to want to change her behavior.

I still recall my mother's touch, voice and kiss as she put me to bed. This memory is a blessing of peace and love that has continued with me all of my life, one that I tried to give to my own children. Now I see them passing it on.

The Bedtime Blessing

Bedtime needs to be, and can be, a time of blessing and peace for our children. When they close their eyes at the end of the day they need to know that God loves them, Mommy and Daddy love them, today is finished, and tomorrow we will begin again...and in their little world, all is well.

Now the day is over, night is drawing nigh,
Shadows of the evening steal across the sky.

When the morning wakens, then may I arise,
Pure and fresh and sinless, in your holy eyes.*

BUILDING BLOCKS

☐ A little game to play at bedtime is "The Best and the Worst." What is the worst thing that happened to you today? Now, what is the best thing that happened? It is usually wise to start with the "worst" and end on a positive note, with the "best." This provides your child with an opportunity to talk about anything that may be on his or her heart before going to sleep, and it also teaches them to end the day with happy thoughts. If you have a very sensitive, anxious child, you may not want to even bring up the "worst," but only focus on the "best." This is also a game that can be played at family dinner.

☐ Psalm 121:3–4
He who watches over you will not slumber;
indeed he who watches over Israel
will neither slumber nor sleep.

---

*"Now the Day Is Over" by Joseph Barnby.

Enjoy Them!

- Geri -

> However many years a man may live,
> let him enjoy them all.
>
> Ecclesiastes 11:8

When I get married...*then I will be happy.*

When I get a great job...*then I will be happy.*

When I own a home...*then I will be happy.*

When I have a baby...*then I will be happy.*

When the baby sleeps through the night...*then I will be happy.*

When my child begins to walk...to talk...goes to school...*then I will be happy, then I will be able to really enjoy life.*

Then the children grow up, they leave home, and we sit around thinking about "the good old days," when life was really great!

Unfortunately, this is the way some of us look at life. Joy and happiness are always stretching out just beyond our reach. We are waiting for something to happen or to change in our lives before we allow ourselves to be happy. For many people, joy is the ideal which the harsh realities of life keep them from attaining. It will come our way one day, when things settle down, settle out and we can settle in.

I have news for you: Happiness is a choice you make, a choice you can make *today*. One of the most important things we can learn as women and as mothers is to enjoy life *now* rather than later. Mom, go ahead and enjoy the chaos, the exhaustion, the challenges and the imperfection. Accept and embrace this time in your life *now* because it will pass more quickly than you can imagine. I promise you, one day, you will look back on these days and long for them again.

Every age and stage of motherhood comes with its unique challenges, and some will be easier to navigate than others. You may be a woman who has more difficulty handling the stress of pregnancy and caring for an infant, but who loves the toddler years. Perhaps you are a natural with preschoolers who are potty-trained and can tell you what they want, but you don't do so well with infants. Whatever your particular strength or weakness, don't waste or lose this special time with your children because of these difficult periods. Instead "roll with" the hard times, and focus on those things that will be the precious memories of your future.

Are you exhausted because of a baby that has you up every two to three hours through the night? Do you feel like a walking zombie? Perhaps so. If you wish, you can choose to think only of how bad you feel, the sleep you are not getting, and *when* will this end.

Or, you can decide to treasure these times in the darkness of night when the house is peaceful and it is just you and your precious child, alone together. Tell me, which way of thinking is the best for you?

There will be different challenges throughout your life. Just when one difficulty passes or you have learned how to handle it, another emerges. There will always be something that can steal your joy and prevent you from enjoying your children and your life. I urge you—don't let that happen. Here is an invaluable lesson I have learned: Enjoying life in the present keeps me from having regrets as I look back at my past.

I don't want you to be a mom who one day looks back and wishes that you had enjoyed your children more. I don't want you to wish that you had laughed more, played more, hugged more and had more fun. Instead of seeing only your troubles and problems, see the precious, the funny, the beautiful and the poignant moments that are taking place every day right before your eyes. Cherish this time; squeeze all the enjoyment out of it that you can!

My mother loved raising her four girls. I remember hearing her say many times as we were growing up, "*This* is my favorite time!" I would love to tell you that she enjoyed raising us because we were all such obedient, perfect children, but I cannot. There were times when I know we made her cry, that we disappointed her, and times that I know she was utterly exhausted and exasperated...but above everything else she was thankful for her husband and children, loved being a mother, and took the time to enjoy us and to enjoy her life.

She carried this attitude with her after we were grown. When her life changed after we left, she continued to enjoy it. She enjoyed her grown daughters and the relationship she had with us as adult women. She enjoyed the husband she once again had all to herself. She now loves being a grandmother and a great-grandmother. She is eighty-eight years old, and she still enjoys her life!

You see, enjoying life is dependent upon an *attitude*, not a *situation*. Learn this lesson now while your children are young, and you will not one day look back with sadness or regret. Instead, as you go forward to the next stages of your life, you will embrace each one as positively and as fervently as you did the last.

Enjoy Them!

Sometimes I call Elizabeth or my daughter-in-law, Lisa, and they can hardly finish a sentence without being interrupted by something happening with the kids. Questions, cries, giggles, running feet, banging sounds.... You know, I really don't feel sorry for them. This is the one of the greatest times of their lives.

The other day Sam phoned our son-in-law, Kevin, and upon hearing lots of noise and racket in the background, asked, "Kevin, just what is going on over there?"

Kevin's answer? "The kids are climbing all over me!"

Does it get any better than that? I don't think so. *These* are the good old days! Enjoy them, and enjoy them right now!

BUILDING BLOCKS

☐ As you lie in bed tonight, take a few minutes to remember and relive some of the best moments of this day. Even on your kids' worst days, there are still moments of sweetness to treasure. What toddler antics made you laugh? Did your child reach a milestone? Did you get a spontaneous hug or butterfly kiss? Fix those precious moments in your heart and mind, and thank God for the priceless gifts of motherhood.

☐ Ecclesiastes 8:15
So I commend the enjoyment of life, because nothing is better for a man under the sun than to eat and drink and be glad. Then joy will accompany him in his work all the days of the life God has given him under the sun.

I Wonder

Elizabeth Laing Thompson

Midnight dreams dance behind eyelids delicate as paper, fluttering.
Tic-tac toes wiggle and splay, stretching.
Slender fingers tremble and interlace, praying.
Rosebud lips twitch and purse, shaping a tiny O—

And suddenly, a ray bursting through clouds—
You smile, even as you sleep.
I melt.

"Just a reflex," says the knowing cynic,
Peeking over my shoulder.
"Gas," nods another.

But I wonder:
Do you know what I do not?
Do you hear what we cannot?

Do angels hover near newborn ears,
Telling jokes,
Making promises,
Granting blessings—
Whispering?

Bright eyes blink open, just for a moment,
Their nascent blue radiating the wisdom of ages
In an all-knowing stare meant just for me.
You wink.
And I wonder.

Guardian Angels

- Geri -

For he will command his angels concerning you,
to guard you in all your ways.

Psalm 91:11

Have you ever wondered how God does all the things he does and how he can do so many things simultaneously in so many locations? The greatness of God is truly mind-boggling, and yet, as great and all-powerful as God is, even he has help. The Bible tells us that God has angels who assist in his work, "ministering spirits sent to serve those who will inherit salvation" (Hebrews 1:14). I don't know about you, but for me, that is an exciting thing to think about!

Angels have been delivering messages and carrying out God's plans from the beginning of time. They go where God tells them to go and do what God wants them to do. When God sent Moses to deliver the Israelites from Egyptian slavery, he used his angels to orchestrate the ten great plagues. When the coming birth of Jesus was announced, God sent his angel Gabriel to deliver the message, first to Zechariah, then to Mary, and finally to Joseph. Later, when the baby was born, a host of angels filled the sky, singing praises to God. And when Jesus was praying in anguish in the Garden of Gethsemane, an angel from heaven came and strengthened him. Angels are awesome beings, mighty and powerful servants of an almighty God.

Even more incredible for me as a mother is the knowledge that God has such a special love for children—mine and yours—that he actually watches over them with his angels! When Jesus spoke of little children, this is what he said: "See that you do not look down on one of these little ones. For I tell you that *their angels in heaven behold the face of my father in heaven*" (Matthew 18:10, emphasis mine). "Their angels"! As parents we cannot be everywhere at once and, try as we might, we cannot protect them all of the time. We do not have to. God sees what we cannot see, and does what we cannot do. His angels are watching over our children.

But in spite of these promises, we still hear stories of terrible things that happen to small children. The network of instant worldwide communication can really frighten us. We seemingly can't turn on our televisions without learning of another tragedy or receiving some warning of some new, sinister danger. The result is that, more than ever, mothers are worried, anxious and afraid that some calamity might befall their children.

How are we to think about this?

First, we must remember that in spite of God's protection, we are not promised a life free of difficulties, sadness and heartbreak. Bad things do sometimes occur, and can happen to good people who serve and trust in God. For those of us who have experienced the pain of the illness or even the loss of a child, we can only turn to God in such times, knowing he does indeed work everything out for our good (Romans 8:28).

But it would be a terrible mistake to live with a constant, gripping fear that life is out of control, and that random fate could cause something terrible to happen to our children. Instead, we can take heart in the fact that God has commissioned each of our kids with their own personal angel to watch and stand guard over them.

I have often said that I think we wore out several of God's best angels keeping up with our four children! Each of our kids was delivered from at least one near-death experience— and that does not include all the times God's angels were hard at work, preventing things from ever getting dangerous to begin with.

When Elizabeth was about four years old, two strangers drove up in front of our neighbor's house where she was playing in the front yard. Her young playmate had gone back inside his house for a moment, and she was all alone outside. The strangers opened the car door, and the woman in the passenger seat called Elizabeth over and invited her to go for a ride with them. Our daughter later told us that she actually placed one foot on the frame of the car door while they spoke to her. But while they were talking, Elizabeth remembered that "Officer Friendly" had just visited her school that day and told the children to never get into a car with a stranger. She politely declined their invitation and moved away from the car.

When we found out, we called the police, who told us that they had received other reports of a car of that same description approaching a number of other children in the area. I have often wondered what angel had sent Officer Friendly to her school that particular day...or perhaps reminded Elizabeth of his words of warning!

When we lived in Miami, our sons Jonathan and David often climbed in a large sea grape tree in our back yard. The branches were sturdy and low to the ground, and the tree was easy to scale. Our boys had been in the tree often, and without any mishaps. One afternoon we were having a big

Fourth of July picnic and Jonathan, who was about seven at the time, was perched on a branch in the tree. We heard a loud cracking sound and turned in time to observe the branch snap, and our son plummet about ten feet toward the ground.

Horrified, we saw him land on his back on the edge of a concrete picnic table. We ran to his side, and as he writhed in pain, we helplessly waited for the paramedics to come. We prepared ourselves for the worst possible news; we thought he surely would be paralyzed for life. Miraculously, he was fine; nothing was broken or ruptured. It was as if God sent an angel to break the fall, cushioning the landing just enough to protect him, but also to teach him—and us—a good lesson about climbing trees.

The most humbling and frightening experience I ever had as a mother, and the one that most convinced me that guardian angels are at work, was when our youngest daughter, Alexandra, was seventeen months old. With a family of four children there always seemed to be a lot of busyness and confusion, and this day was no exception. We had recently moved to Miami and were preparing for an activity at our house that evening. I had just arrived home with the children and dropped them off to stay with their dad while I drove to pick up pizza for a hurried dinner.

Somehow, in the confusion of unloading everybody from the minivan and leaving the house again, Alexandra toddled out of the front door—unseen by anyone. I started backing out of the driveway, not seeing anything behind me. Then I "felt" something. I stopped, and then I heard crying. I got out and found my baby, knocked down, crying and lying behind and just underneath the van. She was scratched and scared, but unharmed.

I need to tell you that I didn't stop crying for three days! All I could think of was what *could* have happened, what *almost* happened. I have always wondered: How could I have "felt" my bumper come in contact with a small child of twenty-two pounds?

Sam later told me that at that same moment, he had a sensation come over him that Alexandra was in danger, and he ran out the front door looking for her. I believe deeply that something or someone stopped me, and also alerted my husband...an angel? I don't know all that goes on in the unseen world, but I do know that God graciously allowed us to keep our daughter and see her grow up into the beautiful young woman that she is today. It could have been so different.

With our son David, there is no one story to tell. Instead of any individual scary moment, I think David challenged the angels every day of his young life with all of his adventures and mishaps—resulting in several concussions, a number of stitches and knocked-out teeth.

As I write this, I am reminded of the continual grace of God and his faithful vigilance. All I can say is that God obviously had a plan for my children's lives, and his angels worked overtime to keep them here in one piece to bring it to pass!

Does all this mean that we have a guarantee that no harm will ever come to our children? No, I am afraid not. But we can know with certainty that our kids rest safely in God's arms, under the watchful eyes of their guardian angels. We must also know and accept that God is the one who created us all, and that "all our days were written in his book and planned before even one of them began" (Psalm 139:16).

In other words, if something does happen to one of our children, God is still God. There is a plan at work that we may not fully comprehend, but that in the end, will always prove to be a good one. He is still watching with his angels, and as difficult as it is for us to grasp with our limited human understanding, God has a greater design for our good, one that we may not see today or ever figure out in this life, but one that we can trust and embrace.

I have a dear friend who lost an infant to SIDS (Sudden Infant Death Syndrome). Several weeks after her baby died, a neighbor shared with her something unusual that had happened that terrible day in the hope that it might comfort her and her grieving husband. She spoke of watching the ambulances and the paramedics arrive at their apartment to minister to their stricken child. When they wheeled the baby out, the neighbor's three-year-old daughter pointed toward the stretcher and said, "Look, Mommy! There's Jesus!" Might it be that children, in their innocence, are able to see what we, with all of our supposed maturity, are unable to see?

My friends lost their only son that day. They suffered an unimaginable loss, but they also believe deeply that their baby is safe and happy with Jesus and the angels. For reasons they will never fully understand, his time here was very short, but they are comforted by the fact that one day they will see him again.

Mothers, may we live with a great sense of peace and calm as we raise our children. We are to love them and care for them as best we can, but we are limited. Do your best to keep them safe and protected, but please, relax. Don't let fear and anxiety keep you from enjoying this special time in life. You are not alone in caring for your children. Your Father in heaven is there to help you.

Never forget that all of us have been given life by God, and that we are sustained by him. His angels are everywhere—watching, guarding, protecting! All the days of our lives are in his hands. Let this give you comfort and peace.

BUILDING BLOCKS

☐ Take a few minutes to reflect on times in your life when you were protected from or saved from harm. Perhaps it was a person who came along at just the right moment, or a series of events that did or did not happen. Although we do not see God, he is always there and always working for our good. Take some time today to thank him!

☐ Zephaniah 3:17
The LORD your God is with you,
> he is mighty to save.
He will take great delight in you;
> he will quiet you with his love,
> he will rejoice over you with singing.

Saved Through Childbearing

- Geri -

And we...are being transformed into his likeness with ever-increasing glory, which comes from the Lord, who is the Spirit.

2 Corinthians 3:18

I am glad I was born female! Because I am a woman, I have been able to experience the thrill of carrying and bearing children, of seeing my own body change in ways that I never thought possible as it housed and fed a growing, living being. I will never forget the feelings of a baby kicking and moving inside me or the miracle of seeing my babies for the first time as they entered the world. And I have never gotten over the miracle of watching them grow up and change.

I saw my baby girls develop into beautiful young women and my little boys become handsome men with deep voices. Miracle upon miracle, every one of them, every day.

Although the birth of her son was an event unique in all of history, I can still relate to Mary as she sang,

"My soul glorifies the Lord
    and my spirit rejoices in God, my Savior,
for he has been mindful
    of the humble state of his servant.
From now on all generations will call me blessed,
    for the mighty one has done great things for me—
holy is his name." (Luke 1:46–49)

Saved Through Childbearing

Like her, I have experienced the miracle of bearing children and the blessings of seeing them grow to adulthood.

But as a mother I have seen seemingly countless other miracles take place in my life. Just as I watched in awe as my body grew and changed through pregnancy, I have seen the "inner me" change. These changes usually took longer than nine months, and many of them were slower to be evident, but change I did. And I am continuing to change.

I believe that raising our children changes us as nothing else in life. It exposes weaknesses in our character, such as selfishness, fear and anger; and it drives us to God for help. Many of us probably never knew we had a temper until our two-year-old challenged us. Others of us were confident and sure of ourselves until we tried to outsmart a three-year-old. And we haven't even begun to talk about the challenges of the teen years! Nothing will more expose our flaws or show us our need for God, and nothing will more soften our hearts and build our faith.

I remember how many times I read and clung to the verse: "But women will be saved through childbearing, if they continue in faith, love and holiness with propriety" (1 Timothy 2:15). I took great comfort in the knowledge that as I hung on faithfully to God and his ways, I was being molded into the woman I longed one day to become. Some days I wondered if raising kids was taking years off my life, but mostly I was thankful that motherhood was making me into a better woman. I was learning to be more unselfish, more patient, more understanding. I was learning to love more deeply and unconditionally than I could have ever imagined.

As my children grew older, I learned to entrust them to God and to "let go." Today my kids are grown up and I am a grandmother, but I still have not arrived! I have so much further to go. But I take heart that I have grown through all these years. It hasn't always been pretty, and it certainly has not happened quickly, but God has been slowly and surely maturing me and molding me into someone who is a much better representation of himself.

Motherhood is one of God's greatest miracles and our great privilege, but it certainly is not easy. There will be days when you are exhausted, times when you are unsure and insecure, hours of chaos and confusion, and moments when you are tested to your limits. But during those times, know that God is with you:

> He tends his flock like a shepherd:
>> He gathers the lambs in his arms
> and carries them close to his heart;
>> *he gently leads those that have young.* (Isaiah 40:11, emphasis mine)

You may not feel it; it may be difficult to see—but in all of this, God is very much at work, molding you into the person you one day will be. Remember that God is not yet finished with you—you will be amazed at who you will become.

BUILDING BLOCKS

☐ Take a few minutes today to think about the ways that being a mother has already made you a better person. Now, take some time and try to picture the person you hope to become in the future.

Saved Through Childbearing

☐ Romans 5:3–5

We also rejoice in our sufferings, because we know that suffering produces perseverance; perseverance, character; and character, hope. And hope does not disappoint us, because God has poured out his love into our hearts by the Holy Spirit, whom he has given us.

Different Pace, Same Passion

- Elizabeth -

> Therefore, as we have opportunity, let us do good to all people, especially to those who belong to the family of believers.
>
> Galatians 6:10

As a campus minister's wife, I sometimes read to single women the scripture in 1 Corinthians 7:34–35 that says,

> An unmarried woman or virgin is concerned about the Lord's affairs: Her aim is to be devoted to the Lord in both body and spirit. But a married woman is concerned about the affairs of this world—how she can please her husband. I am saying this for your own good, not to restrict you, but that you may live in a right way in undivided devotion to the Lord.

I encourage the young women to enjoy this flexible time in their lives as an opportunity to serve God in ways they will not be able to when they are wives and mothers. Our young single years are such a fun, exciting, liberating stage of life!

But it doesn't last forever. When we get married, our responsibilities at home make us a little less free to gallivant around town whenever we desire. 1 Corinthians 7 acknowledges that reality! And once we have babies, a seismic schedule shift takes place—a change that can leave us reeling and unsure of how to serve God in our new role.

The temptation can be to stick our head in the ground

and camp out at home, basking in our own maternal joy. Perhaps you have seen the "newlywed fog" steal some of your friends: They get married and disappear into wedded bliss for months or years! Beware the even more paralyzing "baby fog"! It strikes in one of two ways: Some of us are so content and fulfilled in our new role as mothers that we just want to stay at home rocking the baby endlessly; others of us are so overwhelmed that the thought of leaving the house makes us start to twitch. Before long, our friends may begin to wonder if we are still alive.

I have searched for a companion verse to 1 Corinthians 7 for young wives and mothers, and the closest I can find is Titus 2:3–5 (a passage we quote throughout this book):

> Likewise, teach the older women to be reverent in the way they live, not to be slanderers or addicted to much wine, but to teach what is good. Then they can train the younger women to love their husbands and children, to be self-controlled and pure, to be busy at home, to be kind, and to be subject to their husbands, so that no one will malign the word of God.

It is a godly thing for us to devote ourselves to our husbands and children. They should be the first people we serve, and we shouldn't feel guilty about that. It is even biblical for us to stick closer to home. Keep in mind that your children are your God-given personal ministry. Every day, you are planting seeds in their young hearts that you hope will bloom into a lifelong relationship with God.

Since the Bible does not give an abundance of specific direction to young wives and mothers, I have also looked to some women in the Bible for example and inspiration. When I read about Phoebe, a little-known woman from the church in Cenchrea, I knew I had found my role model. I love the way Paul describes her at the end of his letter to the Romans:

> I commend to you our sister Phoebe, a servant of the church in Cenchrea. I ask you to receive her in the Lord in a way worthy of the saints and to give her any help she may need from you, for she has been a great help to many people, including me. (Romans 16:1–2)

What an eloquent, simple description: She was known as "a servant of the church" who had greatly helped many people. I wonder what she had done to aid so many people...but in a way, I am glad we don't know the details. There are countless ways to give; I just want it said of me that I, like Phoebe, am a servant of God's church.

I also draw inspiration from Priscilla, another friend and coworker of Paul's, who worked alongside her husband, Aquila, in serving several congregations, including Rome and Ephesus. After Paul's mention of Phoebe in Romans 16, he goes on to say, "Greet Priscilla and Aquila, my fellow workers in Christ Jesus" (verse 3). My husband's passion and profession is the campus ministry. He works with a group of 120 college students, and although I am not employed by the church as he is, I enjoy serving alongside him as much as I can.

Each of us is able to handle a different amount of pressure and a different kind of schedule. The important thing is not how much we *do*, but how much we *love*—not our *pace*, but our *passion*. I always tell myself that although my schedule is different right now, I want to keep the same love for God and his people that I have always had. I don't live in guilt, comparing my schedule now to what it was before—there is just no way for me to accomplish all that I used to. I do what I can; I try to think outside the box—but I don't feel like less of a Christian just because I can't *do* as much as I used to. We're saved by grace, remember? No amount of good deeds can earn us a spot in heaven!

It starts with fighting to remain close to God—it's difficult to serve him when we are running on spiritual fumes. And when we are connected to God, serving and loving others is a natural product of that relationship; it spills out from the overflow of our hearts.

Ephesians 5:16 and Colossians 4:5 urge us to make the most of every opportunity; I encourage you to be creative in finding ways to serve God and love others—Christians and non-Christians alike. Pray that when you *do* manage to leave home, God will lead you to people who need a relationship with him.

Can you reach out to some of the younger college or teen girls in your congregation, inviting them to come over and play with you and your children? Some of them have never seen a godly wife and mother in action.

If you can't handle making dinner for company, can you invite people over for dessert and coffee? Or do you have friends or neighbors who would want to join you for a Leftover Night? They bring over their leftovers, you warm up yours, and *voila!*—you have a whole meal.

If you are stuck at home with sick children, let your kids help you write cards for friends. If you find the motivation to bake muffins or brownies, double the recipe—there is always some family or friend in need of good comfort food. Or if you achieve the miraculous accomplishment of going to the grocery store, can you call a sick friend and ask if they need you to pick something up for them?

At the very least, we can always serve others in one

simple—yet crucial—way: through our prayers. When I saw the movie "Facing the Giants," I was moved by its depiction of an older man who spent every evening walking through the halls of the local high school, praying for revival among the students. He didn't personally interact with the students, but he did what he could for them: He prayed.

God is not concerned with our actions so much as our hearts; focus on stoking your zeal for God, and the rest will take care of itself. In the meantime, enjoy your days at home in this season of life...it won't last forever.

BUILDING BLOCKS

☐ Who can you pray for this week? Post a prayer list where you will see it throughout the day. Pray with your children, teaching them to pray for friends and families in need.

☐ 1 Thessalonians 4:11–12
Make it your ambition to lead a quiet life, to mind your own business and to work with your hands, just as we told you, so that your daily life may win the respect of outsiders and so that you will not be dependent on anybody.

Bless This Mess

- Elizabeth -

She watches over the affairs of her household
and does not eat the bread of idleness.
Her children arise and call her blessed;
her husband also, and he praises her....
Give her the reward she has earned.

Proverbs 31:27–28, 31

If cleanliness is next to godliness, then I'm going to hell. Or at least my house is. Before I had kids, my house was pristine—sparkling, even—baseboards, tile grout and all. Since baby #2 graced us with his presence fourteen months after his "big" sister, and baby #3 came along only twenty months after that—well, it's all gone to pot.

After spending half an hour taking care of our kids a few weeks ago, Kevin came to me smiling and said, "Being the parent of small children can be summed up in one word."

Warming at his sentimentality, I tried to guess: Fulfilling? Magical? Priceless?

He shook his head. "Gross."

Sad, but true. And that grossness has a way of taking over every inch of your home that isn't covered in Saran Wrap.

When I go to other people's orderly houses—people with older kids, or an empty nest—I want to cry when I think about my own chaos. Sometimes I go to my parents' or my in-laws' houses, sort of because I want to visit with them, but mostly because, secretly, I just want to sit in a neat, toy-free environment that I had no hand in cleaning. (Sorry, Mom, Dad, Bill, Glenda!)

It wasn't always this way—certainly not before I had kids, and not even when I had my first two. When I had just Cassidy, I was able to use her naptimes for serious cleaning—plus, she went to bed at 6:30 or 6:45 every night for quite a while, so I had a good bit of time to myself. Even when I had the first two kids so close together, I quickly got both on the same nap schedule, and then I had a few hours in which to pull my life and home together. Naptimes are God's gift to mothers—his way of keeping the challenges of motherhood from being more than we can bear. If you can get your kids on the same nap schedule, you will give yourself a mother's most precious commodity—free time—and will be able to keep your household running.

Even now, I am still fighting the good fight (admittedly, a different one than the battle Paul referred to in 1 Timothy!). I can't go to sleep at night without reclaiming some semblance of order in our house—a task that often takes a solid hour. I wake up to a clean house, but within three minutes of the first child's nuclear-blast awakening, all my beautiful order is destroyed.

I realize that most young mothers do not have three under three, and so your chaos may not be quite as extensive as ours is—but then again, maybe it is! When you try to juggle working outside the home along with raising even one young child, housekeeping tends to get pushed to the bottom of the list (along with sex...but we cover that in another chapter!).

I may be exaggerating my mess a little—we don't live in a pigsty—but like most young mothers, my entire home is never perfectly clean, all at once. At best, we may get one room or one floor thoroughly cleaned at a time. For those of us who have a bit of the clean-freak in us, this facet of parenting can be disturbing. There is always *something* we haven't done yet. And even when our house is neat, it rarely feels truly, deeply *clean*.

The other day, I had finally emptied every laundry basket in the house—for two magical hours all the laundry was done and my soul was at rest. And then my son woke up from his nap with diarrhea. I'll spare you a description. As I lugged his bedding (which I had just changed the day before) upstairs to the laundry room, I moaned to my husband, "I can't ever get all the laundry done!"

He started laughing and said, "You still don't get it, do you? You will *never* get the laundry all done!" And he was right. I would guess that some of you, like me, have been unconsciously fighting the very nature of laundry and a lived-in house—indeed the very law of entropy—that all things tend to move to a state of disorder.

But we're not crazy for wanting organization. God is a God of order and beauty. In Genesis, we read about the delight he took in "decorating" the universe; in Exodus, we read his intricate design plan for the temple, including detailed instructions for curtains and lampstands. God has created us to enjoy peaceful, lovely environments, and so we should do what we can to maintain our surroundings. When we have kids, attempting to keep a clean and organized home may feel like trying to hem in the tide, but we can't just give up!

I am no Martha Stewart, nor am I an organizational guru, but I have found a few strategies that work for me— Elizabeth's Rules of Order, if you will. You may have different cleaning priorities and standards—this list may seem elementary to some and overwhelming to others—but if my methods help another mother survive, I have not cleaned in vain.

General

Every day I try to do one small thing besides the normal daily maintenance: Clean all the toilets (five minutes); dust one room (three minutes); vacuum one floor of the house (ten minutes); wipe down the stove (five minutes)...you get the idea.

While your kids are still young enough to think cleaning can be fun, let them "help" you! Cassidy and Blake fight over who gets to hold the extra duster and mop when I am cleaning. I figure, why not let them dust and dry mop the floor? They might actually save me a little time.

Laundry

This practice became necessary after my second child was born: wash one, dry one, fold one. Every day, *at the absolute minimum,* I wash one load, dry another load, and fold another. (As my kids get older and their clothes get larger, this minimum number will increase.) This keeps the cycle moving along, so I don't get too swamped. And it's manageable. All together, this strategy means that I spend about seven to ten minutes a day on laundry.

I am a big fan of the dry cleaner for my husband's dress shirts and pants. It's surprisingly affordable (also tax deductible if it's for work clothes, believe it or not!), and the fact is that I just can't iron his shirts the way a professional can. Plus, when can you safely iron *anything* with little ones tugging on everything in sight?

I try to change everyone's sheets within a day or two of

each other (barring bouts of stomach illness, bed-wetting regression, or diaper malfunctions, of course). That way, I don't forget to change a kid's sheets, and I always know that everyone is sleeping on relatively clean beds.

Dishes

I can't stand a pile of dishes in the sink. I run the dishwasher at night, just before we go to bed, so I can get all our late-night snack dishes in there. I always empty the dishwasher while the kids eat their breakfast (translation: while they are busy, seated and sort of happy), so we can start the day with a clean slate and an empty sink.

Toys and Kid Stuff

The amount of junk that a baby ushers into your home is astonishing. And I do mean *junk*: toys, artwork, beloved rocks and dead flowers... If we aren't vigilant, before long we won't be able to find our children beneath their *stuff*! With that in mind, the first rule comes from my ultra-organized mother-in-law:

A place for everything, and everything in its place. If I have a set place for every paper, receipt, toy, doodad, cell phone accessory, and so on, the house gets clean much more quickly and is much less likely to get cluttered. I collect clutter only when I don't know where to put things—so I end up with a pile of junk on the kitchen counter that I don't know what to do with. If something new enters our home, and if it's here to stay, I've got to make a permanent spot for it, so it doesn't float around.

Okay, I don't actually follow this next one—I read it somewhere—but it's a good idea and I wish I did it: When something new comes into your home, get rid of something old to make room for it.

I like to keep a donation box handy, so I can toss in clothes and toys that the kids no longer use; then I can just drop them off at a charity when I'm running errands (I drop off the junk, not the kids—even though it's sometimes tempting!).

I love my kids' crafts from Sunday school and preschool, but I am not sentimental about them. I figure I'll save a handful of artwork from each kid to put in their baby books, but the rest goes to that great Garbage Can in the Sky, pretty much the same day, or after a few days on the bulletin board.

I try not to keep junk toys around for more than a few days, when the novelty has worn off (Happy Meal prizes, etc.). I also usually toss the slew of miniscule accessories that come with toys. I can't have tiny choking-hazard-Cinderella-shoes tripping me up all day long, so until my kids are old enough to (A) keep their toys in a semi-organized manner and (B) fight the temptation to eat their toys, I throw away the extra little pieces when they aren't looking. I feel a little guilty, but my house thanks me.

When I am vigilant about following these rules, our household remains functional and my sanity, intact. Then, as God surveyed his handiwork in Genesis and said to himself, "It is good," at the end of each day I too can look around at my house—my little world—and say to myself, "Well, it's pretty good"...at least until morning.

BUILDING BLOCKS

☐ At least once today, make a game out of clean-up time. You could sing "Whistle While You Work" or pretend you are Mary Poppins tidying up the nursery...or whatever gets your kids excited. Even if your child only puts away one toy, applaud enthusiastically, and enjoy dreaming of the day when you will have eager little helpers around the house. (Okay, maybe *eager* is a pipe dream, but at least they will be capable!)

☐ Psalm 19:1–2, 4–5
The heavens declare the glory of God;
>the skies proclaim the work of his hands.

Day after day they pour forth speech;
>night after night they display knowledge....

In the heavens he has pitched a tent for the sun,
>which is like a bridegroom coming forth from his
>>pavilion,
>like a champion rejoicing to run his course.

When God Is Your Husband

- Geri -

> For your maker is your husband—
> the Lord Almighty is his name.
>
> Isaiah 54:5

Elizabeth was recently alone for a week while Kevin was away taking graduate classes. By alone, I don't mean she had an empty house. Not at all—she was in company with a six-month-old, a two-year-old and a three-year-old twenty-four hours a day! As I observed the constant demands and the practical challenges of running her life and her household, I was once again reminded of God's plan for raising kids: It takes two! God's ideal plan is for children to be raised by two parents—a mother *and* a father. But we live in a world that is not perfect, and for reasons of death, divorce or personal decision, many children are being raised by single parents.

When you are a single mother, it is easy to feel alone and overwhelmed, and to think that you don't fit anywhere. To a single mother, it can seem that the whole world revolves around married couples. Let me assure you that you *do* belong, you *do* fit in. Yes, you have special needs and challenges, but there is a bond that all mothers, married or single, share: the universal bond born of a fierce love and devotion to our children and the intense desire to raise them to become adults of confidence and character.

I urge you to let the principles and insights of this book

speak to you and strengthen you. Yes, your situation is different from others and your challenges may seem greater, but whatever true and godly principles of parenting you see here, adapt and apply them to your life.

Let me offer a few principles to help you with the challenges you may face.

Lean on God

You cannot do this job alone, and you don't have to. The Bible speaks of the special relationship that God has with women who are by themselves. He offers them his special love and care. In a beautiful Old Testament passage God says that "he gently leads those who have young" (Isaiah 40:11). Draw close to God. Depend on him for strength, wisdom and guidance, and for peace and security. He loves you with a special understanding and compassion, and he is there for you.

My sister was a single mother for many years, and I remember her saying what a great husband God was for her. There were times when she didn't know where the money would come from to pay a bill or buy groceries for her family, but it always seemed to come from somewhere. There were times when things broke, and she didn't know how to fix them. She still recalls times that she prayed about broken faucets, appliances (or cars!) and then tried to use them again, and found them working as good as new. God was a very faithful husband.

Being a single mother can be especially hard because of lingering regret or guilt. Perhaps you made some mistakes in a past marriage, and it ended in divorce. Every one of us lives with things we wish we had done differently, but regardless of our past sins or failures, God longs to forgive us and let us start over. We are the ones who won't forgive ourselves, who keep remembering our mistakes and refuse to allow ourselves to go on and live happy lives. Do not allow yourself or your children to live in the shadow of regret or shame. The Bible expresses so beautifully God's desire that we heal and go on:

> "Do not be afraid; you will not suffer shame.
>> Do not fear disgrace; you will not be humiliated.
> You will forget the shame of your youth
>> and remember no more the reproach of your
>>> widowhood.
> For your Maker is your husband—
>> the Lord Almighty is his name—
> the Holy One of Israel is your Redeemer;
>> he is called the God of all the earth.
> The Lord will call you back
>> as if you were a wife deserted and distressed in spirit—
> a wife who married young,
>> only to be rejected," says your God.
> "For a brief moment I abandoned you,
>> but with deep compassion I will bring you back."
> (Isaiah 54:4–7)

It Is Not Impossible

It may be hard and challenging to raise your children as a single mother, but it is not impossible. And it is certainly not impossible to raise them to be strong and spiritual. In fact, some of the greatest men in the Bible were raised without a strong or ongoing father-figure.

I think of Timothy, a young man who grew to be one of the great evangelists and missionaries of the early church. We know little about his father except that he was not a Christian.

He was a Greek—perhaps a Roman soldier—and he definitely was not a spiritual influence in Timothy's life. We do know that the early influences in Timothy's faith were two Christian women: his mother, Eunice, and his grandmother, Lois. It was later in his life that God gave him a father in the faith, the apostle Paul (2 Timothy 1:5, 1 Timothy 1:2).

Another young man who appears to have been raised by a single mother was John Mark, the author of the Gospel of Mark. We see him at different ages: first as a fearful young boy, fleeing the scene at the arrest of Jesus. We later encounter him as a young man serving on a missionary journey with Paul and Barnabas, and finally as a valued friend and help to Paul. (See Mark 14:51–52, Acts 12:25, 15:36–40, 2 Timothy 4:11.) The church in Jerusalem met at his mother's home (Acts 12:12), but there is never any mention of a father's presence in his life.

The greatest hero of all, who probably lost his father at a fairly young age, was Jesus himself. The last time we hear of Joseph's presence was when Jesus was twelve years old, speaking to the Jewish elders in Jerusalem (Luke 2:41–48). Thereafter we read of his mother and his siblings, but not his father. Because Joseph seemed to be a godly and devoted husband and father, we may rightly assume his absence was because of death.

These are but a few of the great men that we have loved, admired and followed who were raised, molded and taught by spiritual single mothers.

Looking at the church today, I see many great men and women raised in single-parent families who became strong, spiritual adults whose influence makes a real difference in people's lives. My husband, Sam, lost his father when he was twelve years old. Because his father was sick for a long time before his death, Sam was never close to him. Although he missed having the influence of a father, he did have a wonderful, strong and devoted mother, a great older brother, and other masculine influences that came into his life when he needed them most.

More importantly, I think his desire for a father led him to develop an especially close relationship with God, and also motivated him to be the devoted father he has been for our children. Our kids still joke about all of the times when after a particularly involved talk with their dad, he would unfailingly say, "Well, you just had one more deep talk with your dad than I ever had with mine!"

Believe this, single mothers: Your task is difficult, but it *is* possible.

You Are a Family

When you are a single parent, it is easy to be so overwhelmed with life that you may forget to do the simple things that create and deepen your ties as a family unit. Here I speak of doing things such as eating dinners together or going on family outings and vacations together. These are the activities that create memories and the feeling of family.

All families need routine and order, but a single-parent family needs it in a special way. Even though it may be harder for you as a single mother to do this by yourself, it is still essential, and it can be done. Your children need a rhythm to their lives. They need to experience the things that you do together that will define you as a family. They crave the memories of family and togetherness that make their life a joy. They need the identity and security that comes with knowing you are, and always will be, a family.

I have recently become friends with a young mother in

our church who just over a year ago suddenly and tragically lost her husband. After his death, she made the decision to move thousands of miles to Georgia with her two sons so she could be closer to family and get a fresh start. I have been amazed and moved as I have watched her deal with her life. She misses her husband deeply and has been very open and honest about this with her boys and with her friends. But, she has been determined to create family for the children.

Recently she packed up the three of them and drove ten hours to Florida where they spent four days vacationing at Disney World. It was the first time she had ever made a journey like that on her own. As I talked to her after their return, I realized that while it was not a perfect or easy trip, it was a great memory that they will have the rest of their lives. And as much as anything, she proved to herself that she *could* do it. In fact, she is now doing things with the help of God she would never have envisioned herself doing.

As I write this chapter, I think of the women I admire who, for various reasons, are raising their children alone. Some of them bear the pain and regret of mistakes or poor choices; others have to live with the hurt of rejection, and others have lost those they love because of sickness and death. All of them have had to deal with intense feelings of loneliness and sadness. But they have learned to lean on God and draw strength from him, and I have seen them grow in ways they had not thought possible.

These women are examples to me of strength, faith, joy and compassion. They have been able to do a job that, in a perfect world, should be done by two people. But, as I think of it, I realize the job *has* been done by two, because they have turned to God, their mighty Father, Husband and Helper.

BUILDING BLOCKS

☐ Think of something that you can do together as a family. It may be that you begin to regularly have dinner together, or it may be a fun activity. Let me encourage you to keep it simple. Understand that this doesn't have to take a lot of time or money. In our family, our greatest memories were not necessarily those events that were expensive or complicated, but were the special times we spent laughing, talking and enjoying being together.

☐ Psalm 68:5–6
A father to the fatherless, a defender of widows,
    is God in his holy dwelling.
God sets the lonely in families,
    he leads forth the prisoners with singing;
    but the rebellious live in a sun-scorched land.

The Big Picture

- Geri -

My son, if your heart is wise,
    then my heart will be glad;
my inmost being will rejoice
    when your lips speak what is right.

Proverbs 24:15–16

I want to share with you one of the great secrets of successful child rearing: *Raise your children to let them go!* God has ordained that we as humans keep our offspring with us longer than any other species in his creation. The reason he does this is so that parents can prepare their children for life out on their own. Since human beings are created with eternity in their hearts, parents have much more to train into their children than just how to survive in the world. We have about eighteen to twenty years to fulfill this vital mission of imparting to them a spiritual understanding of who they are and why they are here on this earth, and it comes to an end far sooner than we think.

Raise your children with an eye to the future. Never forget that every day you are shaping a life; every day you are moving a child closer to the man or woman they will one day become. What kind of person do you see them becoming? Keeping an eye to the future affects the way you live right now—the lessons you teach, the values you emphasize and the character you shape. An eye focused on the future causes us to observe our child's actions and character today and ask the vital question, "How will this look in five years, ten years or in their adult life?"

What do you want your child to grow up to be like? I am not speaking of choosing their profession or where they will live; I am talking about shaping their character and heart. Do you want him to be honest? Then diligently teach him to tell the truth—model honesty and expect it while he is young. Do you want her to be responsible? Then train her to work hard at home and at school now, while she is young. Do you want him to be a loving, caring adult? Encourage him as a young boy to love and to serve others. Teach her that although she is important, special and deeply loved, she is not the center of the universe. Teach him in the days of his childhood to respect authority. Teach him when he is young that life is not always fair and it will not always go his way. In everything you do, you are preparing your son or your daughter for the day when they will live their own lives in the real world.

More important than anything else—do you want them to love God, to be men and women of faith? Then teach them while they are young:

> Love the LORD your God with all your heart and with all your soul and with all your strength. These command-ments that I give you today are to be upon your hearts. *Impress them on your children.* Talk about them when you sit at home and when you walk along the road, when you lie down and when you get up. (Deuteronomy 6:5–7, emphasis mine)

Teach them about God continually, in everything you do! Teach them that God is all-knowing, all-powerful and loves them more deeply than they can imagine. Help them to understand that God is the ultimate authority, and he is the one that Mommy and Daddy serve above anything or anyone else.

I love my children more than life itself, and I loved raising them. I loved every stage of childhood, from infancy to the teen years. But in the midst of every stage I was deeply aware of how quickly my time with my children would pass. At times this realization made me wistful, but mostly it gave me a sense of focus—and a helpful type of urgency. I knew I was shaping a young life that would one day leave me. What did I want them to know and to remember?

Though at times it may not seem like it, your children are *going* to grow up. Who will they be? Look at the big picture, and let it affect everything you do, the example you set, and the things that you teach. Raising kids is about so much more than this urgent present moment, more than just making it through this day. It is about how we use each day to prepare our children for their future.

We certainly know that we cannot rear perfect children. We don't have an absolute guarantee that even with our best efforts we will raise them to become faithful Christians; God has left it to them to make their own adult choices. But, know this: *What you do makes an immense difference.* The teaching you do while they are young—even very young, during the Tender Years—may just be the most profound they will ever receive. Don't underestimate its power. Your words and your example will live with them forever in their hearts and minds, to the end of their days.

Young mothers, keep your eye on the big picture. You can rest assured that the lessons you are striving so diligently to teach and the example you are seeking to set are imparting to your children your own unforgettable message, and that it will never fade away.

> Train a child in the way he should go,
>   and when he is old he will not turn from it.
> (Proverbs 22:6)

BUILDING BLOCKS

☐ Take a step back from the daily grind of parenting, and think "big picture" for a moment. What character traits do you most want to develop in your children?

☐ Proverbs 6:20–22
> My son, keep your father's commands
>   and do not forsake your mother's teaching.
> Bind them upon your heart forever;
>   fasten them around your neck.
> When you walk, they will guide you;
>   when you sleep, they will watch over you;
>   when you awake, they will speak to you.

I'm Still Here

Elizabeth Laing Thompson

Michelin-Man legs kicking and flailing,
with a mighty grunt
you heave your roly-poly belly over,
then crane your weeble-wobble head around
to see where I went, though I have not moved—
I smile.
"I'm still here."

Breakfast time, your pancakes wait;
you clamber up to gobble, squealing, "Cake-cakes!"
I sip my coffee on the couch behind you;
you cast glances over your shoulder to find me—
twinkle-eyed, you flash that syrupy heart-stopping grin.
I laugh.
"I'm still here."

First day.
Your thin fingers squeeze mine in a death grip,
but soon you scamper off, hand-in-hand with a new friend;
every so often you pause to take sly peeks
at the pack of chatting Mommies—
I wave.
"I'm still here."

"Here is fine, Mom."
I brake, a dozen yards from the swarm of
bookbag-burdened pre-people.
I turn to hug you, but the door is already shut,
your back melting into the mob, disappearing.
I sigh.
"I'm still here."

A shrill ring jangles me from a noontime armchair nap.
Little shouts and babbles tumble in the background
as we laugh across the miles.
A squeaky lisp interrupts, the line crackles; you chuckle.
"Are you there, Mom?"
I nod.
"I'm still here."   (cont.)

A rattling disturbs my dreamy haze—
my own ragged breath.
A soft hand brushes cool against my forehead,
a lilting voice, warm as honeyed memories, sings lullabies—old friends.
"Don't stop," I say, even as I drift.
I smile.
You whisper, "I'm still here."

Discussion Group Guide

Chapters in *The Tender Years* are loosely grouped based on related themes. This discussion guide is designed for a series of ten discussions, but could easily be adapted for four or six discussions, or for a longer series. You may also wish to incorporate into your discussions scriptures used in the various chapters.

Discussion 1
Introductions, Chapters 1 through 4
Introductions; Who's the Boss?; The Instruction Manual; Mother, May I; Stars, Charts and Princess Dresses

1. Do you find it natural to bring the Bible into your parenting and family life? How can you better use the Bible in practical, daily situations? Share ideas that have worked for you.
2. Are you confident in your parenting? Why or why not? What are the situations in which you feel the most confident? What parenting situations bring out your insecurities? What would help you to become more confident?
3. Do you have one child who challenges your confidence more than others? Explain your answer.
4. How do kids' manners affect their character development?
5. Do you have any ongoing child-rearing dilemmas that have you stymied, overwhelmed or frustrated?
6. Share ideas for creative parenting strategies (i.e., rewards, consequences).

Discussion 2
Chapters 5 and 6
What Quiet, What Time?; Are You There, God? It's Me, Mommy!

1. How are your times with God going? Do you find it easier to read the Bible or to pray?
2. What can you do to build time with God into your schedule again? What tips in the chapters did you find most helpful? Do you have other ideas to share?
3. How can you more literally "walk with God" throughout the day? How can you bring him into conversations with your children? How can you pray more as a family?
4. How can you teach your children to love God and to connect with him, not just to be religious?
5. Why is it important for your children to see you spending time with God?

Discussion 3
Chapters 7 and 8
Sisterhood of the Traveling Diapers; It Takes a Village

1. Why is it helpful to invite other people into your family life?
2. What are your strengths and weaknesses in building friendships? Have friendships been easier or more difficult to come by since you became a mother?
3. How can you draw closer to other mothers of young children?

Discussion 4

Chapters 9 through 11
Still the One; Wife First, Mommy Second; Got Romance?

1. How has parenthood affected your marriage?
2. What do you most appreciate and admire about your husband's parenting? What different sides to him have you seen, now that he is a father?
3. Do you find it easy to work with your husband in disciplining your children, or are you constantly at odds? (Remember, the goal here is not husband bashing!) You can only change one person—yourself—so what can *you* do to work better with your husband?
4. Share ideas for how to foster closeness with your husband during these years.

Discussion 5

Chapters 12 through 15
You Are Special; The Happy House; Smiles and Hugs; Playing Referee

1. Are you a positive person? What kind of mood dominates your home? What kind of mood do you *want* to dominate your family life?
2. What triggers frustration, stress or unhappiness for you (i.e., a busy schedule, a messy house, a sick child, or even a certain time of day)? How can you prepare to handle those situations so that they don't bring you and your family down?
3. How are the sibling relationships going among your children? Are you actively engaged in teaching them to treat one another kindly, or have you backed off or given up?
4. What do you most appreciate about each of your children? How can you teach your kids to appreciate those things about each other?

Discussion 6
Chapters 16 through 19
Superwoman Syndrome; Dream Job; Little Einsteins; Let Them Play

1. How does the world's approach to child rearing, marriage and family differ from God's? How influenced are you by the world's teachings about parenting and family?
2. Are you a guilty mom? What triggers your Mommy Guilt (i.e., your children's education and achievements; the amount of time you spend with your kids; your kids' behavior; the pressure to "keep up")?
3. Take some time to encourage one another in your strengths as mothers.
4. Are you trying to do too much? Is there anything you can or should do to simplify your life?

Discussion 7
Chapters 20 through 22
Discipline Starts Early; 'No' Is Not a Four-Letter Word; Broken Record

1. Where do you begin with disciplining a very young child? What kind of discipline, training or boundaries are appropriate at nine months? Twelve months? Eighteen months? Two years? Three years? Four years?
2. What do you find yourself repeating time and again with your children? How can you tell if you need to change your strategy, or if you just need to persevere over time? Help one another make the distinction.
3. Do you feel bad when you say "no" to your children? Why is it sometimes important to say "no" even when you could say "yes"?
4. What is the most important "house rule" you are trying to establish right now? Why?

Discussion 8
Chapters 23 and 24
Enjoy Them!; Guardian Angels

1. What worries and fears for your children disturb you the most?
2. What helps you to surrender your fears to God? What scriptures give you the most comfort and peace?
3. How aware are you of God's unseen protection? How have you seen it at work in your family?
4. What steals your joy? What—if anything—can you do about those things?
5. Are you taking the time to enjoy this time of life? What is your favorite part about having young children? What will you remember and cherish the most in later years?

Discussion 9
Chapters 25 through 27
Saved Through Childbearing; Different Pace, Same Passion; Bless This Mess

1. How has motherhood changed you? What weaknesses has it exposed? What strengths have you discovered in yourself? What traits do you want to develop?
2. How do you want your children to describe you one day?
3. How is your spiritual life going? Do you feel as passionate for God and his purposes as you did in your pre-Mommy days?
4. What can you do to serve God or his church at this time in your life? Share ideas.
5. Share some of your favorite house-cleaning/sanity-saving secrets.

Discussion 10

Chapters 28 through 30

When God Is Your Husband; The Bedtime Blessing; The Big Picture

1. Is bedtime a blessing at your house? What would help it to be a happy time?
2. If you are a single mother, what is your greatest challenge? How is it going creating a sense of family with your children?
3. What kind of people do you want your children to become? What strengths do you see in each child? What do you already see in their character that will need the most work over the years?
4. Do you focus more on preparing your children for success or for godliness?

About the Authors

Geri Laing is a vivacious woman, full of wisdom and spiritual insight. She and her husband, Sam, have written two books: *Friends and Lovers* and *Raising Awesome Kids—Reloaded.* They have served in the ministry for more than thirty-five years and are currently with the Athens Church of Christ in Georgia. They teach throughout the world on marriage and parenting, and Geri is also an inspiring speaker for women's retreats and conferences.

Elizabeth Laing married her college sweetheart, Kevin Thompson, in 1999. Together they have served campus ministries at Duke, UNC-Chapel Hill, N.C. State, Georgia Tech and the University of Georgia. Now that God and the Turbo Family Plan have granted them a dog and three children in three years, Elizabeth works from home as a writer, editor, diaper changer, laundry service, not-so-gourmet chef, house cleaner, personal shopper, dog groomer, baby wrangler, potty trainer and temper-tantrum-defeater. She is always tired but gloriously happy.

Geri Laing and Elizabeth Laing Thompson
www.juliemoonphotography.com